WHAT DID I DO WRONG?

When Women Don't Tell
Each Other the Friendship Is Over

Liz Pryor

Free Press

New York

*f*P

FREE PRESS
A Division of Simon & Schuster, Inc.
1230 Avenue of the Americas
New York, NY 10020

FREE PRESS and colophon are trademarks of Simon & Schuster, Inc.

For information about special discounts for bulk purchases,
please contact Simon & Schuster Special Sales:
1-800-456-6798 or business@simonandschuster.com

Designed by C. Linda Dingler

Manufactured in the United States of America

10 9 8 7 6 5 4 3 2 1

Library of Congress Catalging-in-Publication Data

Pryor, Liz.
What did I do wrong: when women don't tell each other the friendship is
over / Liz Pryor.
  p. cm.
Includes index.
1. Female friendship—Religious aspects—Christianity. 2. Christian
women—Religious life.
I. Title.
BV4527 .P79 2006
158.2'5082—dc22   2006041300

ISBN-13: 978-0-7432-8631-2
ISBN-10:   0-7432-8631-6

For my mother—who taught me love is something that never runs out, and true friendship would keep me happy all the days of my life.

CONTENTS

CONTENTS

Author's Note

I have changed all the names, places, and other identifying characteristics of people in the stories within the following chapters, except for my own and my family's. My appreciation and gratitude go out to the hundreds of women who took the time to stop and share their hearts and experiences with me.

Prologue

"You can date the evolving life of a mind, like the age of a tree, by the rings of friendship."

—Mary McCarthy

I remember thinking how lucky I was to have found a friend like Maggie. I had moved to Los Angeles from my all-American roots in suburban Chicago. I was positive that not a soul I'd meet would go deeper than the color of her hair, and—boom!—along came Mag, real to the bone. Smart, tough, and my kind of funny. We became the kind of friends women live to have. We spent endless hours contemplating life and love and books and men. I was newly married and she was a budding actress. Our lives were perfectly opposite.

The arrival of my first baby was a thrill beyond what either of us ever imagined. We reveled in the baby's every move. The first time my daughter laughed she was sitting on Maggie's lap. We thought she was choking; we panicked in sync like psychotics. When the baby had her first vaccination shots, Maggie came with me. For days afterward we fantasized about the different ways in which we could kill the wretched nurse who had administered the shots into my little angel's bicep. We shared everything that happened in our lives. From the grandest to the smallest, we were emotionally enmeshed.

Just about four years after we met, I called her on an ordinary Saturday afternoon to see if she wanted to join my pregnant-again self and my daughter at the park, and for some reason I didn't hear back from her. When the third day without reply came and went, I began to wonder. Had something happened? Had I pissed her off? Had the baby pissed her off? Had I done something wrong? Two weeks passed. I finally reached her; she picked up her phone and I said, "Oh, my God, is something wrong?"

She answered quietly and directly, "Not really, I'm just sooo busy."

Deep in your heart, where bullshit can't survive, it's impossible to mistake one woman blowing off another for anything other than what it is. When I hung up the phone with Maggie, I knew somewhere inside me that our friendship was over.

It happens without warning and it hits you with devastating force. Your closest girlfriend, the Ethel to your Lucy, the Thelma to your Louise, stops calling you or seeing you. She has decided for whatever reason to move on with her life and she leaves you to clean up the broken pieces of the friendship. The experience can be as painful as the death of a loved one, and just as confusing as an unexpected breakup with a significant other.

Every woman has experienced a failed friendship, but when it happens we rarely talk about it. Why? For one thing, we have nowhere to turn. The one person we confide in during times of duress is the very person who has left our side. As for husbands and boyfriends, well, we know what little solace they provide in this department. "Maybe she *is* busy," my husband, Thomas, replied when I told him about Maggie.

Women are raised to believe that the conflicts in male-female relationships may never resolve, but that the bond between two female friends is steadfast and impervious to other influences. After all, we don't just make friends; we make friends *forever*. So when our nearest and dearest gives us the cold shoulder and the silent treatment, we're left reeling and confused, overwhelmed by a pain that is both acute and unfamiliar. To protect ourselves, we internalize our hurt feelings, bury the issues deep inside us, and try to fill the hole by focusing our attention on anything but the failed friendship.

The problem is that the hole an intimate friend leaves behind can never really be replaced or filled. It *is* the loss of a loved one, a permanent loss, and in some ways dealing with it can be more difficult than dealing with death because this loved one made a conscious decision to leave your life. A full resolution rarely happens, but it is vital for every woman to try consciously to overcome the experience.

CHAPTER ONE

Maggie:
The Loss That Redefines Us

*"Help us to be ever faithful gardeners of the spirit,
who know that without darkness nothing comes to
birth, and without light nothing flowers."*

—MAY SARTON

The ending of my friendship with Maggie ultimately led to the profound beginning of something much bigger—a realization of the prevalence of these unhappy endings to women's friendships and a need to understand them. However, at the time, I was completely unaware of anything other than the sadness, confusion, and havoc her avoidance had brought into my life.

I felt positive that Maggie and I were not these two estranged women. If our friendship were in trouble, we would have discussed it. Something or someone would be accountable. Maggie would never say, "I'm busy" and be done with it . . . or would she?

I hung on as long as I could to the sliver of hope that the whole thing was some sort of crazy mix-up. In fact I convinced myself after another week had passed to call her one more time. Maybe, just maybe, I was insanely paranoid and we would laugh together at the absurdity of the idea of this friendship being over. I dialed her number, and the moment she answered, I wished I hadn't . . . I wanted to hang up, but instead we carried on a brief swapping of pleasantries. Everything I had felt earlier was validated once and for all. She was done.

Through my wave of nausea, I found the courage before hanging up to ask if she was angry with me about something. I think it was my feeble way of letting her know that I was *on* to what she was doing. She stuck quietly and adamantly to the "busy" thing. My sliver of hope was gone as I put the receiver down.

The part of me that sees a glass as half full recognized that at least the guessing was over. She was done. But I was a mess. Just after I hung up the phone with her I felt the first real taste of rage, sadness, and shame. I think I was angry with *myself* for not having had the nerve to say something more direct, like, "I know what you're doing, you coward. At least admit what you are doing here. Say, 'I break with thee.' Say something." But I couldn't muster up any more to say to her even though, clearly, I had nothing to lose. The emotions of these experiences are tough to explain while you're so close to them—and right in them—which is one of the reasons I wanted to write this book—to help myself, and other women, get clarity and perspective on these murky situations.

For about a year after Maggie broke off our friendship, I felt wretched. It was hard not to keep imagining that I'd said or done some godawful thing of which I was completely unaware. I wracked my brain, desperate to recall any clue, and then moved on again and again to scrutinize my overall character. I would find great faults in who I am, but nothing specific to our friendship.

My sense of personal failure at the ending was overwhelming. I had always fancied myself as being blessed with rock-solid intuition, but this experience had totally blindsided me. I was flailing. Eventually my frustration and question led my head to a place where I occasionally contemplated driving over to Maggie's house, waiting for her to come out, sticking my fist down her throat, and ripping out the reasons she didn't want to be my friend. But I didn't.

Months inched by, and Maggie came to rest as an unsettled memory. She was gone, and I'd accepted that I'd always wonder why. I had my second child, and then my third. Life kept me running, moving every second.

And then something happened. Right about the time I began to shift my role as a mother from dealing with small babies to dealing with little people, when sleep deprivation was becoming a rarity, and I was beginning to recall how I had felt before kids, I noticed that something was different about me.

Something inside felt inexplicably off. I had a nagging feeling in the pit of my stomach, a pit that would come first thing in the morning and slowly fade as the day went on. I had no idea what it was about. Then one day, and through more days, it didn't fade. It lingered and gnawed at me. The more I tried to blow off this feeling, the farther it seemed to make its way in, until finally it was living at the forefront of my everyday life.

I eventually had to take the time to try to figure it out. I searched honestly for an explanation of what was really going on. My investigation led quite easily but surprisingly to my female friendships. An entire *trail* of ended friendships with women ultimately surfaced. A few had ended naturally because they or I had moved away or common interests faded, but this trail revealed numerous friendships that had stopped, with basically no ending.

I pondered this realization for a while. I went over it and over it, but each time it came up the same. Friend after friend, women I'd almost completely forgotten, rose from a hidden place inside me.

After pushing aside my denial and self-justification, and allowing the magnitude of this reality to surface, I had a major insight. The endings to each of these friendships in my adult life had come through some form of avoidance. And not just regular avoidance, but a masterful, calculated, methodical kind—quiet, brutal, and alarmingly effective.

I no longer had to question the meaning of the feeling in my stomach. It was a mass of unaddressed emotion that had accumulated after each unresolved ending with a female friend.

After sifting through as many of these experiences, which I've come to call "unendings," as I could remember, I got to Maggie and her more recent avoidance of me. And I realized that *I* had wrought that same, awful, unfinished, questioning havoc on other women. I was floored, and slightly horrified, that I'd been so completely disconnected from the truth about such a significant area in my life.

I felt then that I must be the only woman on the planet who was this blatantly dysfunctional when it came to ending friendships. If this were a universal issue, if every woman had been stopped in her tracks at one point or another by the ending of a friendship, I would undoubtedly have heard about it. At least a few other women would have *mentioned* it.

Yet I could positively say that this subject had never come up. I had never asked a woman, "How are you?" and heard the response, "Not so great, I'm in the process of being dumped by a very close friend and I'm feeling so sad and kind of ashamed about it." No, I'd never heard anything even close to that.

I came to realize that I'd had a little assistance in accomplishing my massive dysfunction. I even found a little comfort in it.

The act of girlfriends dumping girlfriends is simply void of any guidelines or rules. Neither society nor women have decreed it has to be this way, but there is no protocol when it comes to how a woman should end a friendship with another woman. She is free to behave and act in any fashion, fit or unfit. Not a soul will question her. Like no other situation I can think of, accountability and responsibility simply don't exist.

Maybe the general idea is that if something is never acknowledged, it can't be criticized or judged, and the hope is that it will disappear entirely.

Except in my case. I may have shorted out some wiring, because the experiences hadn't disappeared for me. In fact, they had become unrelenting in their drag on my emotional life and were getting bigger and deeper.

I was sure of only one thing. I'd revealed a truth within myself and could never go back on it if I intended to even kind of like myself in the years to come. My life would be unthinkable to me without the female friends with whom I share so much. They contribute so much of what makes life rich and full. How could I have also not dealt with the endings of other friendships?

Having just scratched the surface of the endings to women's friendships, I began to be consumed with the subject. Since it was taking over my life, I started to write this book. It's not a how-to book, or a book in collaboration with an expert, but one written straight from my heart, the heart of an ordinary woman. I'm not a psychologist or a philosopher. I am not a trained expert in anything except for maybe multitasking as a mother. I'm a regular woman, living her life, raising her kids and feeling strongly that I'm not the only one out there who feels the aftermath of unfinished endings with her friends.

I am the fifth of seven children raised in the heart of the Midwest by a mother who honored and respected her girlfriends as much as she did health, God, and good manners. We were not only taught but were able to watch the profound effects of friendship on our blessed mother. She may have had too many children and never enough time for herself, but she always made time for her girlfriends.

I ended up spending four years on this journey into women's friendships. I got together with groups of women and heard hundreds of their stories. Women eagerly shared and purged their emotions, ideas, and questions with others in these groups and with me. And I wrote it all down. I hounded every expert I could find; I located every printed piece of information on the subject of ended friendships among women. From all this, I wanted to learn about and really understand what happens when we women end friendships with each other. And I also wanted to uncover some common sense for dealing with the pain and the process.

The one thing I learned for sure is that these experiences are universal among women. They transcend age, race, educational background, and socioeconomic status. The stories and discussions that lie ahead in the following chapters represent women from *all* walks of life.

In this book I have attempted to band women together so we can all look clearly at the reality of this phenomenon and try to reduce the pain it causes. Little by little, we might begin to understand and acknowledge the big effect that these experiences have on our lives and on each other.

I have changed all the names, places, and the identifying characteristics within all the stories in the following chapters, except for my own and my family's. My appreciation and gratitude go out to the hundreds of women who took the time to stop and share their hearts and stories with me.

CHAPTER TWO

Lila:

Acknowledging the Truth of What We Feel

I had a real breakthrough in understanding women's friendships when I was at a baby shower for my friend Phoebe. I hadn't known her long and was kind of wishing this shower would hurry up and be over. Sitting alone in a sprawling, shabby chic living room with fourteen other women I didn't know very well, I found my mind drifting from what to pick up at the grocery store on the way home to wondering exactly how the eleven different fabrics that graced the lovely room I was sitting in all seemed to work together so well.

A few women were sitting across from me, cutting long strands of pink yarn that would later be used in a game to guess the circumference of the mother-to-be's belly.

And then, out of nowhere, I heard myself addressing the entire room with the question, "Why do you think that when a friendship ends between two women, it gets no acknowledgment?" It just came out of me. I really did want to know what other women thought about this festering concern of mine, but I was pretty positive this wasn't quite the time or the place to begin asking. Maybe this sweet, Martha Stewart–like group of women would either ignore my question or write me off as a slightly unstable stranger.

I was already planning my escape as silence filled the room. All eyes were on me, I was throwing my sweater over my shoulder quite ungracefully, when a quiet woman in a pink sundress asked, "What do you mean? Like when there's a falling out?"

"Yes," I said. "A falling out, a spat, a tiff, a miscommunication, a major blowout. Why is there nothing, not even a short name or phrase, to which we all refer when for one reason or another, a true friendship has ended?"

The hostess said, "When we end a relationship with a man we break up." And I said, "Exactly, and the whole world acknowledges our pain. Our parents, our friends, society says, *this* is something! It's a breakup. How are we doing? Are we getting through it? Are we moving on? We get set up on blind dates, taken for coffee, and sent cards. As women, we get more empathy and compassion for the ending of a relationship with a man than for anything else other than death or birth."

The pink sundress chimed in again, "Sometimes I think I was more devastated when my best friend and I broke up than I was by my divorce. I woke up one day and the reality hit me: we were no longer friends. This horrible space, confused, angry and hurt, became the place I went when I thought of her. Not only did I feel a lack of empathy from the other people in my life, there was almost an entire lack of acknowledgment."

She got it! The room remained very still as the woman continued. "There was really no one to share it with. I still feel these waves of sadness and I wonder if I'm missing her. The relationship ended so abruptly, for me, anyway. Maybe some kind of closure would have made it easier."

Phoebe's sister said, "Of course it would have. My God, we date a guy for three months, don't even sleep with him, and something about this world we live in forces us to address the ending. Whether you tell him the truth, or you labor over a pack of lies, you have to tell him something. So why shouldn't you have to tell your friend something? That just doesn't make sense."

The female caterer collecting empty glasses said, "Well, somehow, I guess with women, we just move through each other."

"Yeah, and that's fine when that's what it is," I said. "But when you've really made a friend, you know, an intimate, someone you've shared all your stuff with, someone who really knows you in and out . . . one might say the ending deserves some words, some explanation, or for God's sake, some acknowledgment."

Phoebe added, "The other day my mom said, 'Do you

ever talk to Lydia anymore?' Lydia was my best friend for twenty years. Most of you already know that. We sort of broke up or fell out almost two years ago. So I say, 'No, Mom, I've told you we don't talk.' She knows this, she *so* knows this. I've told her the entire story several times, basically begging her to tell me how wrong it was of Lydia, how messed up it was that she never gave me an explanation. But this bizarre denial possesses my mother. She continues to behave as though she doesn't know a damn thing about it."

"Maybe she just *wants* it to be that you two are still friends," said the pink sundress lady.

"Maybe she should listen," said Phoebe. "She and everyone else could start to listen a little more carefully. I don't talk to the one woman in the world who has known me longer than any single person outside my family. I don't even get to *talk* about not talking to her, because people don't want to hear it. Something about all of it is way wrong. Something about all of it makes me feel like there's something wrong with me."

I watched and listened as the women responded to each other. It was so riveting I had to stop myself from shouting with joy. *It's not just me!* Another woman named Abby who had been listening but not participating spoke. "I have, or had, this friend, Bridget. I have an idea of what happened, but I'll never really be sure. I'd known her about five years, I guess. Our kids were best friends, our husbands crazy about each other. I've gone over and over what may have been the cause for what felt like such a brutal slap in the face. No contact, no warning, no nothing. Just, they were no longer in our lives. I think of how resentful I became, having to try and explain it to my three young children and my husband. 'Are we going to see them?' 'What happened?' 'Why don't we see them anymore?' they'd ask. I remember feeling like, *I don't know!* Maybe 'cause I suck and she doesn't like me anymore? What the hell happened, and why am I somehow responsible for the answer? Believe me when I say I asked her. I got right in her face and asked her what was wrong! Nothing, nothing was wrong, except for the way she said nothing. I think when a woman detaches, you know, really detaches, there's no getting anywhere. At what point should you say, 'Fine, whatever'? I mean, you don't beg someone to be your friend. I considered begging her to tell me what the hell happened. In the end it was over. I'd say I think about it way too much. I get nervous when I go places we used to go, nervous I'll run into her."

"Why the hell should you be nervous?" said Phoebe's sister. "She did a shitty, weak thing. I don't know what's wrong with you people. Stand up for yourselves. You run into her, you say, 'Hey, how's it going? Feeling good about yourself? Or is my face an endless reminder of what a worthless, dishonest wimp you are?' That's what I would say."

"Would you really, though?" asked Abby. "I feel like, no matter what I say, or think, or figure, it comes down to this: she doesn't want to be my friend. It's quite simple, really. But I have such a feeling of failure. Sure, I know she did a rotten thing. She should have come to me; she should have had enough respect to tell me. But it wouldn't have changed the part that hurts the most, which is that she'd rather not have me in her life at all. That blows me away. I'm ashamed, and even embarrassed. She just threw me out and moved on."

"Have you run into her?" said the caterer, now perched on the piano bench.

"No, thank God. I fantasize about how I would act. Depending on the day and my mood, the fantasies change. Part of me wants to tell her how low and awful and rude and unfeeling she is, and the other part of me wants to say, 'Hi, how are you?' So I don't know."

"That's *exactly* how I felt with Lydia," said Phoebe. "Same thing. I go back and forth daily. I hate her, I miss her, I'm pissed, I'm sad. I can't get over that she sees me as so replaceable. We have so much history and, for the life of me, I can't imagine what happened to outweigh all of that. She was the only one I never had to go back and explain things to. She was there for all of it. If she had been with me through this pregnancy we would have laughed our butts off at the—"

She stopped suddenly, then continued. "You know, this is not actually what I want to be talking about right now. I'm having a beautiful baby girl in seven weeks and . . ."

She began to weep. The other women in the room offered tissues and comfort. I just wanted to disappear right about then.

And then she said, "Okay, I'm *fine,* I'm hormonal. Stop staring at me. I just can't believe that Lydia hasn't seen me pregnant, that she's not at this shower, that I'm going through this huge, unbelievable experience and she's not a part of it."

Her sister piped up. "You know, more philosophical types would tell you that there is a reason for this, that one day you will come to understand and accept it with love in your heart.

I say this: you are better off. This girl was getting ready to show some true and ugly colors, and I personally find her to be completely self-involved, so be grateful and move on."

Phoebe was rubbing her belly by now and looking over-whelmed. The women began picking up glasses and empty plates.

"God, I'm sorry, Phoebe," I said. "I don't know what came over me. I should never have brought this whole subject up, not here and not now."

"It's okay, it actually felt pretty good to get it out, you know?"

Yeah, I did know. I said, "The truth is, in seven weeks the whole world is going to look so different to you. Imagine now how much you're going to love this baby, then multiply that by a thousand—that's what you'll feel when you see her for the first time. What really matters to you will shine clearly, and the other stuff will fade away. The amazing thing about kids is the truth they bring into our lives. That's what we should have been talking about today."

She looked at me and smiled, "You love being a mother, don't you?"

I do, I really do, but driving home that day, I felt my mind was unsettled. There was such an eager sense in that room when the women were discussing their friendships. At one point they seemed to be wrestling for floor time. I was really eager to tell someone the story of my oldest and dearest friend, Lila, with whom I no longer have any contact. Our story was the first I remembered when I realized I had had other unresolved endings.

"The companions of our childhood always possess a certain power over our minds which hardly any later friend can obtain."

—BUDDHA

I was about ten when I first met Lila. She was more than a year older than I was and the single most incredible girl I had come across in my entire ten years on the planet. I had four sisters and two brothers. Our house was inundated with kids of all sizes and ages all the time, but Lila managed to stand out to everyone. It was her spirit, her love and zest for life, that defined her and remains with me even now. Lila had a contagious passion that excited everyone who met her. The more you were around her, the more you began to see and feel things just a bit differently.

The first time she came to the house, we spent three hours in the bushes under my bedroom window. Lila's identity was attached to Bazooka bubble gum, and it was imperative that I learn how to blow enormous bubbles with it as she could. Ours was a clandestine affair as I was forbidden to even *chew* gum, let alone blow bubbles the size of grapefruits. We met at the park the next day and walked in silence blowing one huge bubble after another. This was the beginning of something I knew deep down I would cherish forever.

In high school, life consisted of Lila's gymnastics meets, football games, boys, and clothes. We were crazy happy and always together.

Lila's sixteenth birthday was around the corner. We had

been awaiting this rite of passage—her getting her driver's license—for what felt like ages. The idea that we would actually be in the front seat of a car together was almost too much to imagine. I anxiously waited at home, pacing my driveway while she went for her test.

After a while, I heard a loud, rhythmic honking in the distance. I ran inside and grabbed two Cokes from the fridge and bolted back out. The music blasted and her arms were waving as she pulled in, sitting like the queen of Sheba in the driver's seat of her father's baby-blue Chevy convertible. We belted the words to the song on the radio and felt the freedom that only a brand-new American sixteen-year-old could ever know. I glanced over at her, and she was doing what she had always talked about doing: she was carefully balancing an ice-cold Coca-Cola between her legs, puffing on a Marlboro, and unwrapping a piece of Bazooka bubble gum, all while driving.

She winked and said, "So who's better than us, huh?"

We drove for what felt like forever, and I knew I'd never forget it. She was my mentor and I her ever-trusting best mate, with whom she felt safe and loved. She guided and protected me. Together we defined the flawless female dynamic. No competition, no hidden agenda. We were so specific to who we were when we were together, it was as close to perfect as girls can get.

Lila fell in love the next year, and so did I. It just happened that the guys were brothers, bad-boy brothers, troublemaker athletes who didn't have a care in the world about where they would go to college or what they would do with their lives. We had a blast, and drove our parents slowly insane.

My Lila memories are amazingly vivid, small chunks of life, imprinted indelibly in my mind. Lila grew up in a huge old home on Lake Michigan. The feeling of a long time ago lurked in every crevice of that house, which could have been a beach front inn when originally built. Her room was perfectly placed on the water side of the house, with enormous windows hanging like pictures over the lake.

On one particularly cold, dead winter afternoon, Lila and I and a few of our group were gathered in her room, bored out of our minds. She suddenly had an idea that got everyone fired up: she would pierce my ears! I was the only girl in the room without pierced ears, thanks to my father's firm commitment to keeping his five daughters untrampy. Pierced ears and gum-chewing were tacky and forbidden. As the needle stabbed my poor earlobe and caught the potato on the other side, my father's face flashed before my eyes and I let out a yelp that surprised even me. It took me three weeks to get up the nerve to let Lila pierce my other ear.

Meanwhile, I had become completely obsessed with covering my pierced ear at family dinners. Weeks after Lila had wounded my second ear, I was sitting at the dinner table, forgetting about covering up.

My mother quietly addressed me, never looking up from her plate. "When did you have the holes put in your ears?" I froze. My father hadn't heard her; I quickly shoved my hair in front of my ears and cleared my plate.

Two weeks later my parents announced they were getting divorced. The only thing I could deduce about not having been decapitated for the piercing was that they were completely preoccupied with the breakup of their marriage.

When Lila left for college, I thought quite simply that I would die. I had no friends my age. Going to school was torture for me. When you've spent three straight years hanging out with the girls a year older, and then they leave, it's not a good thing. The girls my age shunned me like a leper.

My senior year of high school was a lonely challenge. The other girls had become like teenagers in a horror movie. My life was friendless and lonely. Maybe it was payback for my not having taken any interest in them the previous three years. Whatever it was, I didn't tell Lila that life was coming down hard on me until the end of the school year, but as soon as I did, she came straight home.

Lila arrived at my graduation and stood like a quiet guard next to me. Every single one of my female classmates who had taken such joy in my solitude that year was momentarily silenced by her presence. She made my exit for me, and I would forever love her for that.

What freedom I felt when we walked out of that gymnasium, me in my long white dress, diploma in hand, and Lila with all that made her Lila! We walked together, and without saying a word we both knew we were never coming back to live in that place we'd called home.

In time we found ourselves loosely planted at opposite ends of the country. With new jobs and lives in the real world, our contact began to wane. The phone and an occasional holiday visit home defined our communication. Yet the friendship didn't skip a beat. We were locked somehow; time, change, space, it didn't matter. We would forever be what we had always been, till we were old and older.

I was sitting alone in my studio apartment one day when the phone rang. It was Lila. She said she was calling just to chat. For the very first time, I heard something in her voice I had never heard before. There was something meek about it. A faint sense of self-doubt that seemed to linger behind everything she said. I remember thinking after that phone call, what was *that*? I was suddenly the voice of wisdom and strength, feeding her confidence and direction. I completely overanalyzed it, and came up later that evening with an answer. Changes happen, maybe I had changed, maybe Lila was going through something, or maybe I was hallucinating.

She came to town a few weeks later. I made it a point to prove to myself that the phone call had been a fluke. I opened my door, and there she was. Without her opening her mouth, I could see something was different. We sat on the bed with the four walls staring at us. At first it was strange, and then she was Lila. We reminisced and smoked cigarettes and drank wine. The next day I went to see the house her new boyfriend had recently purchased. A few days later she was headed back East. I asked her if everything was all right. She assured me she was great. Time passed, and the "amiss" remained. Months after our visit, I received a postcard from Italy: "Max has proposed, I'm getting married! Will call soon. Love you, Lila."

She was getting married. Her boyfriend, whom I'd met maybe twice in my life, had taken her to Italy and proposed.

I was by her side for five full days before the wedding. We prepped and primped and pampered and talked. I tried to put it all together in that short period of time. Lila seemed almost a shadow of herself. Just the same, we devoured every moment we had. I was standing next to her when she said her vows. She was stunning, poised, composed, and without gum.

There should be a distinctive adjective for a wedding like Lila's. It was colossal, on the grandest scale. As I worked my way through the crowd of people, having said my good-byes, I took one last look at her. My memory froze that frame. I caught her eye and waved, and then I left.

About a year or so later, I myself was to be married. Lila and I had been talking less and less. It was a brutally busy time for both of us. We had arranged to meet at one point in New York City and she never showed up. That's how distant things had become. After a good amount of denial, I pushed most of what I felt about Lila far away into a sort of interior storage closet where I put things I didn't want to feel but couldn't throw away.

I saw her arrive at my wedding. We spoke briefly, with some degree of discomfort.

One of my sisters came to me shortly after that and told me Lila was leaving. "You should say something to her." As I turned in her direction, I saw her struggling with her coat and saying good-bye to some of my siblings. She headed toward the door, and I just watched her.

That was the last time I ever saw or spoke to Lila. I wrote her a letter a few months later. I told her all that she'd meant to me and how much I wished we wouldn't lose each other. I said in the letter that I was sure our lives would be filled with different people, husbands, children, friends, but that she and I would always be what we'd always been. I never heard back from her.

A couple of years later she saw my husband being interviewed on television. He was talking about the recent birth of our daughter Conner. She decided to call and say congratulations. I never called her back.

Ten years passed. We never had a confrontation or discussion. The ending is floating out there with the millions of other unendings.

After reliving these years by writing down this story, it dawned on me that I'd never before told or even thought through the truth of this experience. I frankly couldn't believe that I had allowed this to happen. I'd *like* to say that life is busy. Getting married, having children, growing older, trying to make life work become all-encompassing. There was no good time to go back and fix Lila and me. One big fat distraction after another can allow anyone to justify pretty much anything. Our story was so hard to look at, but it was even harder to let go of all the bullshit I had created about how not having my oldest friend didn't affect me. It did. The fact that Lila was not in my life is tragic. But finally being able to look at the truth behind it has helped me.

The question I'd posed at the shower about lost friendships had created such a stir. I'd heard a lot of stories out of the blue. The women spoke about their ended friendships with a sense of desperation. They were dying to purge, to tell, to claim, to deal with the emotions. When I got home after the shower, in fact, I had a message from Phoebe, who left me three phone numbers of women who had also been at the shower and wanted my number. She was sure it all had to do with the girlfriend conversation.

I was in it now, all the way in it. These women felt what I'd been feeling. This wasn't just validation—it was proof.

So I started my research with my close circle of intimates, questioning and interviewing. Then I moved on to cousins, friends, neighbors, and acquaintances. Finally, I found myself approaching everyone and anyone I could find who was female, random women standing in line at the car wash, at the grocery store, in the carpool line. I spoke with nurses, waitresses, nannies, and grandmothers. Birthday parties, soccer games, and the local park were my meatiest sources for stories. My style was unconventional, but it was effectively revealing a widespread problem.

After several months, I had created a little buzz in this small dot of a place I call home. I was the woman around town writing the book on how women end friendships. I received numerous phone calls every day from friends, and friends of friends, and sisters of friends of friends, pretty much total strangers to me. The women all wanted to purge and share and confess their emotions about the lost and forgotten friendships in their lives.

We're not alone in the pain, sadness, and confusion that follow these experiences. Here are our stories. Maybe you will be helped by hearing them and find one that is similar to your own. And maybe you'll decide, as I have, that you don't want any more unendings in your life.

CHAPTER THREE

Finding Our Own Way:

Unexperts and Unendings

The power of our girlfriends, the magnitude of girl-talk, and the bonds that tie us so deeply to one another have finally begun to interest scientists. Still, there is not a lot of published information we can refer to as we try to find our way through unexpected endings. Shelly Taylor, a neuroscientist at UCLA, states, in the September 2003 *Los Angeles Times* Health Section, "Rigorous study of women's friendships remains in its infancy, but scientists are beginning to respond to the 'wake-up' call."

In fact, we do now have scientific proof for what women have felt for centuries: our friendships are important. And they protect us from the hardships of life. The quality of our lives and how long we live are directly affected by our girlfriends. At the beginning of 2005, a health study from Harvard Medical School found that "the more friends women had, the less likely they were to develop physical impairments as they aged. And the more likely they were to be living a joyful life. In fact the results were so significant the researchers concluded that not having close friends and confidants was as detrimental to our lives as smoking or obesity."

In "The More Social Sex," an article published in *Newsweek* magazine, Anna Kuchment writes: "Wherever you look, female friendships are portrayed as frivolous— significant only to the sappy parties involved. But 'girl talk,' it turns out, isn't quite so trivial after all. Scientists are finding new evidence that women's friendships and communication have played a crucial role in human evolution. Female ties have evolved to ensure that certain vital functions important to life get maintained."

In a special *Los Angeles Times* women's health section, staff writer Melissa Healy beautifully states,

Women are keepers of each other's secrets, boosters of one another's wavering and confidences, co-conspirators in life's adventures. Through laughter, tears and an inexhaustible river of talk, they keep each other well, and make each other better.

Across species and throughout human culture,

females have banded together for protection and mutual support. They have groomed each other, tended each other's young and engaged in the kind of aimless sociability that has generally mystified male anthropologists.

For women, friendship not only rules, it protects. It buffers the hardships of life's transitions; it lowers blood pressure, boosts immunity and promotes healing. It may explain one of medical science's most enduring mysteries: why women on average have lower rates of heart disease and longer life expectancies than men.

We don't need science to tell us what we know is so magnificent. But friendship's importance also underscores that we need to pay attention to a friendship when something is going wrong. Women's love and commitment to one another is abounding, yet when friendships end, we show little to no respect or honor for that which has enriched, supported, and even prolonged our lives.

I now see the way we end friendships as an opportunity for growth. All of us admit to the significance and importance of our friends, so as we yammer on and laugh our way to great health, there must be a way for us to notice that these unacknowledged endings don't fit. They don't make sense. I am convinced all we need to do is to look at it together.

We cannot be powerful as individuals or as a group if we don't support and honor our friendships all the way through to the end.

At the beginning of my quest for expert advice on women's friendships, I was pretty frustrated, unable to unearth much. I got up one morning and staggered to the front door to retrieve the paper. When I reached down, cursing the bright sun in my eyes, I found instead a magazine with a Post-it attached that read, "Read this." The magazine was one that I never buy but always peruse at the grocery store. The typical headlines on the front cover included: THIN THIGHS IN THREE DAYS. TEN WAYS TO ADD MEDITATION TO A STRESS-FILLED DAY.

And, in fancy red letters at the bottom of the cover, HOW TO BREAK IT OFF WITH A GIRLFRIEND.

I was scanning the pages looking for the article when my phone rang. "Hello?"

"Have you ever read such crap?"

"I didn't get to it yet."

"Yeah, well listen to this." It was Cara, one of the first great women friends I had made when I arrived in Los Angeles. Cara and I had lived a lot of life together when we were single in Hollywood; she was maid of honor at my wedding and is godmother to my firstborn. She can make me laugh so hard I get mad at her.

Our friendship began when we were in identical places in our lives, and has remained through changes that could so easily have ripped it apart, yet we have never even teetered on the brink of breaking. We remain rock solid, I think because we met at a time when neither of us had the nearby support or love of our families or other friends. We were both new to a daunting city, but quickly learned that our background was incredibly similar, although we hailed from different parts of the country. When we described our fathers to each other, for instance, we could have been talking about the same person. Our parallel sensibilities brought us a familiar comfort. Both of us needed a touchstone, another person to help remind us who we were and from where we came, and how to determine the good, the bad, and the questionable. Cara and I became as close as sisters. Our history has helped hold us so tightly together, but we also leave room for errors. Neither of us will ever be perfect, and both of us have the freedom to be who we are, with the knowledge that the other will accept and forgive. As Charlotte Brontë wrote, "A true friend is someone who thinks that you are a good egg even though he knows that you are slightly cracked."

Just about a year ago, Cara purchased the house two doors away from me, a stone's throw away. She seemed a little unsure when asking me how I felt about it, but I was ecstatic. Since her recent move, our friendship had rapidly become like Lucy and Ethel.

She was yelling at me now. "Are you listening to me, Liz?"

"I'm listening. Go, what?"

Cara began reading from the article on how to break up with a girlfriend in her best sarcastic British accent: *"Explain that your life's journey has taken you in different directions and that you've drifted away from some of the interests that had come to define the relationship. This is not a judgment, simply an observation; it is the inexorable movement of life."*

"Who writes this stuff?" she blasted.

The article notes that it was written by a practicing ordained minister and psychotherapist. We both started to laugh. She was at my door two minutes later, sporting faded workout wear, with our newspaper, coffee, and magazine in hand.

Without skipping a beat she announced, "Only a person who has never in his life been in the shoes of a woman going through an ending of a friendship could have written that." I sat down to read my copy while she flipped through hers.

The reverend's article refers to the ending of a friendship and, through its five major points, defines the process of breaking it off. But ending is not downshifting, I thought. It really is ending, terminating, closing.

The reverend's points are the guidelines a woman might want to follow when pursuing a downshift: honesty, inventory, inevitability, economy, and sadness. His economy point seems most clueless about women and advises that a woman should share with her friend how little time she has in her life to spare. And how that makes it difficult but necessary for her to *apportion free time more frugally."*

Under "Inventory," he suggests a woman make an actual list of the reasons the friendship was so valuable to you in the past—presumably to keep it ready and available as the downshifting progressed.

He discusses at length a one-on-one conversation, to allow for eye contact and observable facial expression. Most of the women I'd spoken with about ending friendships would find this scarily close to what we call confrontation. The reverend further offered that, *"One person's hand placed gently on the other's [adds] richness to the communication."*

Although no doubt well intentioned, the reverend's advice is shockingly off the mark for most women and, I believe, for me. In theory, I could see why a man would think these five points would make sense, but we women all need a realistic approach.

The article inspired me to seek out more information from other experts. I ended up spending quite a few days in the downtown Los Angeles library, where I located seven articles published in the last two years, all written by counselors or professionals of one sort or another. I devoured them, searching for hard information, some reasons behind the devastation that had resulted from losing my friends. Yet everything I'd read was laced with trivial, casual lightness. It almost felt as if the writers were dealing with an entirely different subject altogether. I actually got up to wash my hands, for fear this attitude might rub off on me. I was personally offended by a headline on one of the magazines: QUICK AND EASY FRIENDSHIP-ENDING TIPS.

Friendship-ending *tips?* What a shallow way to put it. The women we're talking about are not acquaintances at the bus stop or assigned roommates we can't stand but learn to live with. These are people we had chosen at some point in our lives, friends with whom we made memories, with whom we shared stuff that matters. Maybe over time they had changed and now bug the hell out of us, or they had had kids and become freaky Stepford wives, or had had a lot of plastic surgery and become unrecognizable to us. No matter, moving on and away from these people cannot be addressed with quick tips. Quick tips are for hair removal and growing tomatoes. How could all the experts treat this subject as if they were dealing with a nuisance? This was a subject for commiseration and serious exploration.

Even more offensive to me, the friendship-ending tips are in the form of multiple choice.

> After having decided you do not want a friend in your life anymore, should you,
>
> A. Call her up and tell her you're thinking about moving away.
> B. Meet her for coffee and explain the reasons you cannot continue the friendship.
> C. Slowly stop returning her phone calls and hope she gets the message.
> D. All or any of the above.

The answer for this question appears upside down on the next page as D.

Occasionally, when something doesn't make sense to me I'll find myself drifting into what I refer to as my "conspiracy paranoia." I actually wondered, as I finished my library research, whether there were an age-old, worldwide pact between academics and psychologists to treat women and their friendships as something not terribly profound or significant. Nothing I read seemed to acknowledge the ending of a friendship between two women as anything more troubling than having a bad day. It began to seem as if the subject had been whitewashed and that women in turn had become accustomed to ignoring or dismissing it, too.

But I couldn't ignore it. I felt as if we women were like the king's subjects in the old folk story "The Emperor's New Clothes." They were going along with the crowd and not admitting that something was wrong. I felt like the kid who noticed the emperor was naked and said so, to everyone's embarrassment.

Since the experts weren't helping, I decided to search for explanations from real women. I also wanted to see if the women whose stories I was gathering would have the same reaction as I had to the small amount of advice and research I'd accumulated. Maybe they could make more sense of it. I orchestrated informal group discussions to meet at my house. I had a tape recorder, some food, drinks, and a few couches. The group would provide multiple stories, and the women would be able to commiserate, which would help them gain perspective and not feel so isolated.

My family and I had headed to Connecticut for the summer that year, so my first group discussion would be held on the East Coast. As I was scanning my phone messages, writing down the numbers and names of the people who were coming, I recognized a voice I hadn't heard in a long time, from a woman I'd known fairly well as a child. A gem of a person, she is one of the nicest people on the planet, and has been that way since she was a little girl—

kind, gentle, and totally unassuming. Think Princess Diana.

Her message said, "Hi, this is Jessica, I was . . . well, I heard you're writing a book and you're looking for women to have discussions about their friendships. I'd be very interested in coming to something like that."

It was so out of character for Jess to have left this message, I actually triple-checked the name to make sure it was she. I immediately returned her call and invited her to join us.

The women all arrived around the same time. Jess looked a little nervous and worried as she made her way in. I introduced her to a few people and watched her get settled. I'd tried to make the group as diverse as possible. I didn't want too many people who knew each other very well, for fear it would turn into a gab session about "how's life?" As it turned out, none of the women in this first group knew each other at all.

My friend Rooney, who lives in L.A. and had been very helpful in finding me women to interview, was in New York on business around the time of this meeting and decided at the last minute to come to Connecticut. She *had* to be a part of the first group discussion, out of curiosity and for moral support, she said.

When Rooney arrived, she plopped herself in the most comfortable chair in the room and began thumbing through one of the articles I'd laminated and placed neatly on the coffee table for everyone to peruse. By then, there were ten articles in all, and I was curious to see how the women would respond to them. In fact, I was dying to find out if they got more out of them than I had.

Rooney clanked the ice in her diet Coke, and was the first

to speak up. "Did anybody see this article, written by a reverend and psychotherapist guy? He says here, 'When ending a friendship, women first need to draw a visual map of their boundaries, and then address those boundaries with their friend.' Do you think this is written for women on the planet who don't exist?"

The guests all started grabbing articles off the table, and there was a lot of moaning and hushed laughter. About a half an hour went by as they scanned and swapped the articles. I was getting ready to ask questions and take notes about which, if any, of these experts might have represented accurately what women actually felt about friendships and how to end them, but within a few moments there was a unanimous decision that none of the information came even close to speaking to the truth of what we go through.

Rooney had been dutifully listening to one woman quoting sarcastically from an article, when she lifted her glass to get everyone's attention and asked, "Why don't we move on from reading the amateurs to discussing it with us professionals, eh? When my friend Liz here first approached *me* about this subject, I have to admit she threw me. I was shocked to find that, yes, I, the almighty confronter, had experienced this—endings that were more like nonendings. More like gradual exits, gradual declines. I remembered a few and it was definitely unsettling to me, big time. And then a few weeks after Liz had broached the issue, a great old friend of mine began a quiet exit from *my* life. I would never have been on to it so quickly, if I hadn't already been digging through my past.

"I immediately felt the onset to the ending of this friendship. It was slow and easy, with carefully launched avoidance. I sat back and watched as she quietly stepped out of my life. After enough unreturned phone calls and delayed dates, I confronted her. I point-blank asked her. It wasn't so much the reasons I wanted so badly, but an admission or an acknowledgment that she was bailing. Stubborn as she is, my friend would not admit she was weeding me out. Straight to my face but not quite in my eyes, she spouted all the reasons she'd been avoiding me, none of which included that she was finished with our friendship.

"I drove home after my confrontation, upset and spewing venom at the same time. I waited several weeks; you know, the obligatory time it takes for the friendship to pass to its new form. While I was waiting, I came up with this great term for what I was going through, 'Interim metamorphous-ising hell.' It's the period of time you wait until you can redefine yourselves as women who *used* to be friends. I didn't see anything in any of the articles here on the table that might have helped me get through this debacle more easily. Am I wrong, Liz? Is there anything here that even remotely touches on what goes on? Has anything even been mentioned about the fact that this kind of thing can make the dumped friend feel like a huge loser, and how that might affect her self-esteem? Anything like that?"

"Not really," I answered. "Most of these articles talk about the subject in a way that makes you feel like there might be something wrong with you for feeling so emotional. They give practical tips for confrontation, what and how to approach our friends, but nothing touches on the why's or emotions of it all."

Jessica asked if I had ever read anything about a group of friends dumping another woman. At that time, I hadn't yet, so she began telling her story.

Jessica, her husband, and their three young children moved to a small town in Connecticut from Dallas, where they'd spent most of their lives. Her husband, Jack, had been offered a job he couldn't refuse, but Jess's expectations for life there were pretty low. She was leaving her roots, her family, and all her friends, and felt daunted.

Her arrival, however, was cushioned by the fact that she adored her new home. She described her neighborhood as the perfect mix of traditional and eclectic.

Within a week of moving in, she had met four neighboring families that seemed to have a great thing going. The women were stay-at-home mothers, their children and Jessica's were close in age, and Jessica liked them all.

Pretty quickly, these neighbors became the center of their lives. The children got along, the men got along, and the women had great times together. The routine of their life soon included Friday night pool parties, cocktails, dinners, and fun. The children were happy and busy with each other; even the babysitters for the families were part of this happy circle. They convened for different day trips. They met at a different house daily. Jessica became really close with two of the four women, and she made a point of telling the group how blessed she felt to have their friendship.

As we listened to Jessica, hanging on her every word, her situation seemed so ideal it could have been a setup for an Aaron Spelling TV show. But we all were scared about where it was going.

Jessica carried on in a soft voice. "One morning, about two and half years after we'd moved to Connecticut, I woke up to a tugging at my bedspread. I opened my eyes to see one of my young twin daughters standing over me, sobbing.

"I sat up and asked, 'What is it?'"

"Adela says we can't play again ever with Rachel and Sam."

"I noticed my son standing at my bedroom door, also crying. He spit out, 'I'm never ever allowed to go to Jeff's house.'

"I had no idea what was happening. I went downstairs and asked my live-in babysitter, Adela, what they were talking about. She was also acting strange; she threw her arms up and spoke in Spanish, which I only understand when spoken slowly. I asked her to slow down, and she proceeded to tell me that the kids had called the two neighbor families (as they did every morning). The mothers had asked to speak to the sitter and told her not to allow the children to call the house anymore.

"I said, 'That's ridiculous. Did something happen?'" Adela threw up her arms again. I got dressed and walked over to my closest friend's house, three doors down. When she answered the door she barely opened it.

"I asked her to let me in, and she abruptly said, 'Just go for now, Jessica.'

" 'No, I won't go for now, what is going on?' I demanded. She shut the door tight, and I stood there staring at the closed door. I walked over to my other friend's house, and she didn't answer her door. I called all four families three times that morning. No one answered.

"That evening, my husband, Jack, came home and I told him everything. He assured me that it was a misunderstanding and said he would call my friend's husband at work the following day.

"My friend's husband wouldn't take Jack's calls that next day. So when he came home from work he went over there himself. He asked me again if I was sure I could think of nothing that had happened to provoke a response from these people. I was more than sure.

"He returned quickly with nothing. He said the husband spoke to him briefly and told him this was really something they should discuss another time, but that it was substantial, and he would get back to him on it.

"I was standing in my living room shell-shocked. I took it all out on Jack; I was mad at him for not demanding an explanation. He was as flustered as I and stormed out of the room.

"The next several days were like living some sort of nightmare. Emptying my garbage, watering my flowers, pulling into my own driveway, opening my front door all became daily responsibilities I dreaded. I had a habit of walking nightly with the kids; we would normally hook up with two of the mothers and their children. They now walked ahead of us and made sure their children didn't speak to mine.

"After about a week, the tension was so high in my own house that I thought I was going to explode. My kids were angry and confused and acting out, our babysitter wasn't looking me in the eye, and my husband had become quiet and disconnected. The dropping off and picking up at pre-school was suddenly a fate worse than death for me. I was invisible to my four closest friends. I actually came face to face with one of them at the school gate one morning. I smiled sadly at her and said, 'Pam, talk to me?' She brushed past me and shook her head.

"After a few weeks of this nightmare that had become my life, I decided to search for anything that might help me through this. In fact, don't laugh, but I had read almost every article on Liz's table here before today. One article there talks about confronting the people who disappear, which is precisely what I tried to do, but they literally wouldn't open the door. I searched the Internet, the libraries, and the bookstores for anything to validate how I was feeling about what was happening to me. Nothing came close. I was convinced there was something wrong with how this experience had affected *me*. I was borderline depressed, I think. My life as I'd known it was upside down, with no glimmer of hope of getting back to normal. Finally, my sister, to whom I'd been speaking daily, insisted I call a shrink. I was so depressed and confused . . . I thought it couldn't hurt. But I didn't get in to see the guy for three more weeks and by then I was like a walking zombie. I had no friends. My kids were constantly upset and wanted to play with the children on the block. My husband's antisocial behavior and lack of patience were at an all-time high. The weekends were quiet and strained and hollow for all of us."

Jessica's story was almost unbearable to hear. Rooney asked angrily, "What kind of people are these women? I'm tempted to say you're making this up. This is the worst thing I've ever heard. I didn't even have to help my teenage daughter deal with such ghastly behavior."

Jessica sat fairly composed and continued. "After a few meetings with the therapist I felt myself slowly coming back. I started to feel like I could take a bit more charge over my life. Jack had come around; he was as supportive and as compassionate as I could hope. Seven of the longest months of my life had passed. I tried to regroup, I struggled desperately with the kids, and then finally I decided to put our house on the market."

My new summer neighbor, Jackie, spoke up. "You moved out of that fantastic house you loved so much?"

"Well, what's a house when you're living in hell?" said Rooney.

Every woman in that living room said she couldn't begin to imagine how difficult this must have been for Jess. I even thought that there *had* to be another side to this story. Something must have happened to catapult that group into such abhorrent behavior. Why would those women turn on Jessica and ice her in a single day?

I asked Jessica if she ever found out what happened. That part of her story was even grimmer.

About a year after the icing, before their house had sold, one of the four neighbors finally contacted Jessica. She called late one night and said, "I just want you to know that what's happened with you was not my doing. I know what good people you are, and I'm sorry this has happened." But before Jessica could say anything, her former friend hung up.

A couple of days later, Jessica received a phone call from her former preschool teacher, who said she wanted to tell Jess everything she'd heard about Jessica's family. She felt it was the right thing to do. Jess sat and listened . . . in horror.

Apparently one of the nannies in the circle of families had misconstrued an incident that occurred with the children on the block. One of Jessica's twin daughters had taken off her underpants inside the community's public changing area at the beach while with another little friend. The housekeeper who saw them both turned the incident into allegations of sexual foul play within Jessica's home. The housekeeper told her employers and those neighbors contacted the others, as well as the preschool and all the people in the community who knew Jessica's family to spread this slander.

After hearing the story from her former teacher, Jessica immediately decided to contact all the names she'd been given to try to clear her family's name. Upon her request, the local parish, the day-care center, and the beach club board questioned her entire family. Official apologies came a few months later from the parish, the day-care center, and two well-known physicians in the neighborhood.

Two out of the four neighboring women subsequently called, and wept their guilt and shame for having been a part of something so abominable, but Jess and her family moved from their home soon after the drama ended. She was visibly distraught after having shared this story but told us, as private a person as she had always been, she felt strongly about sharing her story in hopes it might bring the truth out into the open of what a travesty like this can do to someone's life. I later came to find that Jess's story wasn't as uncommon as we'd all thought. However, her particular experience does seem to be in a dreadful category all its own.

In fact her story reminded me of an experience one of my little sisters had in junior high school. All the girls in her grade made up a horrible evil story about her and then told all the other kids and walked around whispering and teasing her. They shunned her for the entire year. Our family could do little to help her, and watched as a team of twelve-year-olds crushed her heart. One night I overheard my mother in my sister's room, lying in the bed with her, trying to ease her sobs of pain.

My sister said, "I just want to grow up, Mom, and then stuff like this won't happen."

My mother said, "Sweetie, life is filled with stuff like this. Growing up doesn't stop bad things from happening. Life just hurts sometimes."

I hated hearing that. I remember kicking the floor and thinking that's not true, you grow up and people aren't mean to you, 'cause you're all grown up.

Yet there we were in Connecticut, eight adult women over the age of thirty, listening to the same heartless cruelty that I'd heard for the first time at twelve years old. There are swarms of books out now on mean girls and this kind of relational aggression, including *Odd Girl Out* and *Queen Bees and Wannabes*. Yet, Jessica was the odd *woman* out on her block—bullied, intimidated, and genuinely suffering.

Rooney pushed herself out of her chair as Jessica's story came to an end and said, "Well, I think we'd all agree, the only thing worse than a heartless woman is a pack of heartless women." She headed for my wine cabinet, filled a glass, and then made a toast. "To Jessica, for making it to the other side with a smile on her face."

Our meeting had gone on far longer than we'd intended. I saw the group to the door and put the last dishes in the sink. As I walked through the living room to the messy pile of magazine articles, I wondered what the reverend would think of Jessica's story. Would he have suggested his five major points to the four women who turned on her? Could *any* of these experts who had written about tidy ways to "downshift" or end friendship understand Jessica's torment? Clearly, solutions to the problems with ending friendships lay elsewhere, not with the professionals but with the real women themselves.

CHAPTER FOUR

Dear Jill:

An Alternative to Avoidance

The discussion groups at my house allowed women to be open about a subject they would not otherwise have discussed. We validated each other's feelings and also offered ideas for coping with ended friendships and alternatives to avoidance as a way to end them. I was committed to holding as many groups as I could.

One night, when Thomas and I were out to dinner, I ran into my friend Grace, whom I've known for more than ten years. She and her husband, Sammy, are old friends of Thomas's from when he lived in New York. Grace could never be mistaken for anything other than the actress she is—she oozes charisma.

When she spotted me across the restaurant she shouted, "Oh, my God, I was going to call you. Ask Sammy, I just said, 'I have to call Liz.'" She ran over, threw her arms around me, and sat down at our table. "I wanted to call and tell you this story. You remember Shay, right?"

"Yeah," I said. We'd both met Shay at our kids' preschool. A quiet sort of retro California type, Shay would definitely have appealed to the homespun, closet-hippie side of Grace. They had begun spending time together fairly often. Their sons enjoyed each other, and had become fast friends.

"Right, well, I can't tell you now because it deserves a true sit-down."

"What do you mean? You don't see her anymore?"

"No, we're done, and it's quite a story. How long ago was I at your house for that group discussion thingy?"

"I don't know, three months maybe?" I said.

"Right, well things were beginning to brew around that time, and then it hit the fan."

Grace had come to my second discussion group. I had invited her because I love seeing her, but also because she's so open. Grace told the group that she has no difficulty whatsoever confronting women in her life, because in her early adulthood she had faced what she referred to as the *ultimate* female confrontation—with her mother. She told us she'd received a letter from her mother that stated unequivocally that her greatest disappointment in life was her only daughter . . . Grace.

Talk about quieting a room. It was one of the sadder things I'd heard in a long time; as a daughter and mother I couldn't fathom it. And I was blown away that Grace, of all people, had been the object of such meanness.

Yet there wasn't an ounce of sadness or malice in Grace's account, and in an odd way we were all reminded of how lucky we were and how much harder and tangled our lives could be.

After reading her mother's letter, she'd wept for days, wallowing in self-pity and anger. And then she picked herself up and sought help. After a year of facing the truth of her life, Grace bought a plane ticket, flew two thousand miles, and arrived unannounced to confront her mother. With forgiveness in her heart, she decided to continue her relationship with her mother. She said that good or bad, right or wrong, crazy or not crazy, you only get one mother in this lifetime. "She's the only mother I have, and I need a mother more than I need to hold onto all my anger." Grace will always struggle to accept her mother for who she is, but feels great resolve in her decision to keep the relationship alive. Grace had gotten herself up and made her suffering pass. She was living proof that what makes us who we are in the end is not what happens to us, but how we choose to live through it. It reminded me so much of something my father used to say to me when I was a little girl and finding life really hard. He'd ask, "What's the difference between a really good woman and a great woman?"

He'd taught me to answer through the sobbing, "How she handles the really bad stuff." Grace was a great woman, no doubt in my mind.

I called Grace a week after seeing her at the restaurant and we decided to meet at her favorite coffee spot, so we wouldn't be distracted by our offspring. I arrived right on time and spotted her sitting at a window table. I sat down and pulled out a file with her name written across the side in big red letters.

She laughed when she saw her file on the table. "What does it say in there about me? What a case I am?"

"No, it says what a hero you are," I said and ordered my sparkling water.

Grace took a sip of her steaming latte and told me to hang onto something and listen.

Babies grow rather quickly into little people, but when they're young, you don't just drop them off at a friend's house and call it a day; you have to accompany them. While your little person plays with his friend and learns socialization skills, you are basically stuck with the play date's mother for up to two and half hours. Technically, you are on an adult play date yourself, but with a stranger you didn't actually choose to be part of your life.

I don't remember hearing about this ritual when I was pregnant and busy preparing for my new life. I was told that I would cherish my kids' young years and meet fabulous new people who would have children the same age, but I never heard about the need to weed through the funky mothers.

A good number of the lost friend stories that I'd heard in the discussion groups had taken place around this time, many more than I would have guessed. I, too, had struggled because of that early kid time, but through it had also met some of my favorite people.

"I liked Shay when I met her," she said. "I don't know a lot of cool and interesting moms, and maybe I was a little eager to meet one. We started hanging out when the boys became friends. We had quite a bit in common. I mean, I had a clue she might be a little wacko, but I've been known to enjoy a bit of a wacko from time to time. But it wasn't long at all before I knew this was not going to work.

"I came to realize that I would not choose to hang out with this woman. Yet week after week I'd find myself trapped in a kitchen listening to her yammer on about her life, and the more she yammered the more I couldn't stand it. I am totally repelled by negativity in people, maybe because I fight so hard within myself to remain positive, to find the good when the bad is so thick.

"She'd sit in my house and just rant, on and on about the horrible state of her life. Just when I'd think there couldn't possibly be one more thing that sucked for her there'd be something else. She'd leave, and I'd feel spent and whipped from the efforts I'd make in trying to find the good. It got to a point where I had no choice, I had to stop seeing her; she was simply bad for me and for my life.

"So, I did what I had to do, and I'll have you know, I felt totally justified in doing it. I thought about it and decided that she and I never really crossed the line to friendship, technically. I mean, we were solely associated through the children; I'd never had a drink or a coffee or for, that matter, been alone with her. So a slow and steady avoidance was the perfect choice.

"I didn't want to sit down with this woman and tell her that her mere presence was unbearable. So I ditched her. Didn't return some calls, said no thank you a couple of times, figured the boys would see each other at school, and that was that. And I swear to God, even Sammy noticed a difference in me. I was normal again. I didn't have to fret under the black cloud of angst she'd dump on me every time we were together. About three weeks after my liberation, I received a message on my phone machine, and it was brutal. Sammy was in the room with me when we heard Shay's voice. She started out sounding really cold but calm, and then she escalated to this angry, loud, emotional maniac. She just ranted on about how rude and insensitive I was. How *dare* I avoid her phone calls, and the audacity of me to think I could just ignore her. Shame on me for dragging our innocent sons into something that was clearly between two women. At the end she said, and I mean venomously, that she would not be ignored and avoided, and was demanding an explanation."

"Jesus," I said. "What did you do?"

"Well, I was shocked at how angry and hurt she was. I mean, clearly my gauge of our closeness was way off of her gauge. The first thing I did was go to my son, to make sure I hadn't screwed up in that area. Her message made me think I had possibly dragged him through my own stuff; I wanted to make sure he wasn't missing his friend. I asked him if he'd been playing with Shay's son at school, and he told me yes. I then asked him if he wished we could see him more, and he said no, playing at school was fine. So *my* son was, as I thought, totally fine.

"Sammy went bonkers. He wanted to call her himself and rip her in half. I told him I'd figure something out, and he told me to think fast 'cause she sounded like a psycho who wasn't going away."

Grace stopped for a second and looked at me. "Can you believe this?"

"Well . . . it's a *little* funny," I said, "that you're dealing with someone who is kind of like you—like you in the way that she's confrontational. So what happened?"

Grace reached down and fumbled through her purse, pulled out four crumpled-up pieces of paper, and handed them to me. "This is what I did and I saved the rough draft for you." I took it from her and read.

Dear Shay,

I am so sorry that you feel so rudely mistreated by me. It was never my intention to hurt your feelings. I suppose there are only two ways to tell someone that you are not interested in pursuing a friendship with them—avoiding them or being honest and telling the truth.

I felt that our relationship was more of an acquaintance, and so I thought I could slip away unnoticed. I think we met at a time in your life when you were deeply unhappy. The pressure of three small children, troubling finances, a four-year ongoing remodeling of your home, and the strain of your marriage is a tremendous load to bear, but for better or worse, it was your creation.

You complained endlessly about the stress and pressure and I must admit it made you a very hard companion.

You didn't share your joyful parts, and I didn't know you well enough to slog through the tough stuff. So I chose to avoid you. I suppose I could have been honest from the start but then I'm sure you would have thought I was really rude.

I hope that your life is easier for you now and that you've gotten to reclaim and embrace all of the best parts of yourself.

It's my mission daily to try and focus on what is right in my life, what works and what brings me joy. Some days I am more successful in seeing this than others, but that is the challenge.

So there it is. I'm sure you don't like it but it's what kept me avoiding you. I wish you the very best with you and your family and if we run into each other I hope it will be a pleasant exchange.

Sincerely,

Grace

"I think it was a great idea to write her a letter," I told her.

Grace ordered another latte and then said, "Well, I wasn't exactly expecting what came next." Shay had written a three-page letter back in response to Grace's, which arrived priority mail two days later.

Her letter began by saying that Grace must have been mistaken, because Shay had never intended to pursue a close friendship with her. On the contrary, her desire to get to know Grace was merely an attempt to support the friendship of their boys.

The letter went into a detailed description of Shay's perspective of what it was like to be around *Grace,* describing her as self-involved and narcissistic, that the joy that Grace had so desperately claimed to feel was contrived and more difficult to be around than she could imagine. Admitting her own unhappiness at times, Shay offered in the letter that at least her behavior was from a true place within herself.

After slamming Grace's integrity and character, Shay ended the letter by stating that she was willing to look past all of this as she feels they are both decent mothers, and would like the boys to be able to continue their budding friendship, which was her intention in the first place.

I finished the letter and started to fold it. This whole situation felt quite a few steps away from most of the stories of avoidance I'd heard. These were two very confrontational women, who appeared to get a little caught up in blame and criticism in their letters. However, the idea of the letters still seemed one that I could imagine might work as an option for simple avoidance.

Shay stated at the end of the letter that she'd like to continue a relationship with Grace. There was in fact a direct invitation. However, Grace never even *considered* responding to Shay's letter. Grace was done, *way* done as she described it. She never spoke to or saw Shay again. The preschool ended soon after, and the two boys went to different kindergartens.

"Okay," I said to Grace. "So clearly you didn't feel any lack of closure or craziness that the whole situation was up in the air again. What *did* you feel after you read her letter?"

"Honestly, I was angry about the constant references to my self-involvement, and I most definitely believe she intended those references to hurt me. Which only confirmed what I already knew. She is a terribly unhappy person. If I've learned one thing in this crazy life of mine, it's that I am in charge of who I let in to be a part of *my* short blessed time here on this earth. The day I decided I would not be around her anymore, she became a memory waiting to be forgotten. Nothing she could have said or written would have changed that. I was out and done and elated about it."

Months after Grace had given me the letters, I called her to ask her some questions and was surprised to learn that she was far more bitter about the letter exchange than she had been at our coffee. She regretted having gotten sucked into what she referred to as the drama of it all. When I asked if she had to do it all over again what she would do, she said she would have ignored the blasted phone message and never written a letter.

Grace's letter to Shay was loaded with opinion and criticism. As much as the purging was truthful to Grace's experience, it would be difficult to imagine anyone not feeling the need to respond. Shay's reactive response was understandable, as she felt the need to defend herself, but she also fell into the trap of accusing and criticizing. Yet, tellingly, after criticizing and pointing blame back at Grace, Shay found a way at the very end of the letter to leave the door open to some sort of relationship. Grace of course was completely closed to the idea.

These two women most definitely let it all out in their letters. Unfortunately it didn't exactly have the outcome Grace had expected. Had she really only wanted to cast Shay out of her life, it might have been more effective to write a different kind of letter, one less loaded and apt to backfire.

Another story involving a letter kept me thinking it could be an effective way to resolve an ending even when the women had been good friends, unlike Grace and Shay. Blake, who lives just outside of Indianapolis, told me about a friend she'd made in her neighborhood a couple of years ago. She and Annette met in a gourmet cooking class at the local college. They started talking and realized they lived just a few blocks apart. Blake described their friendship as "fast and furious." They had so much in common that their budding relationship was at full throttle within weeks.

"We started hanging out all the time. We drove to class together, we jogged in the mornings, Annette often stopped by in the afternoons and would stay into the night. Our daughters were the same age, *and* we shared the most serious kind of passion for cooking . . . and eating. Before I knew it, we were having many dinners together; our husbands worked late and we'd find ourselves lounging and chatting for hours at night. Time passed quickly; Annette was incredibly entertaining."

Blake described Annette with what sounded like a bit of infatuation when they first met. "I admired her toughness, and her sense of who she was. Annette was the kind of woman who could not care less what other people thought, and I admired it. She got more from, and out, of people than anyone I'd ever seen. Food, parking spots, tickets to shows—anything she needed. I once mentioned to her that there was a two-year waiting list at the elite day-care center in our town. The next day she showed up at my house with nametags for our daughters to begin the following *week*. Something about being around Annette made me feel puffed up.

"But there was more to her. You know the old saying,

'Beware of fascinating people'? One morning while we were jogging together, Annette, out of nowhere, started lambasting this man for not having his dog on a leash. It was totally shocking. Her temper flared from zero to ten in five seconds. It scared the living daylights out of me. I joked around with her afterward and said I'd be sure never to make her mad. These little bursts slowly became the other part of Annette, and somehow at the time I didn't register them. The terrific side of her was really seductive. The little red-flag incidents continued, but clearly I didn't pay enough attention."

Blake told me that certain things about Annette's life just didn't add up quite right. When I asked her what, exactly, she told me that for example, Annette lived in an apartment building just a few blocks away from Blake's home. It was the only apartment building in the area, and when they first met, Blake had thought it a little odd that Annette drove such an expensive car, and had such nice things, but lived in this tiny apartment. She described her thoughts about this as fleeting.

Meanwhile the two friends were busy mapping out their daily runs, shopping, and eating fabulous meals together. Annette brought Blake to incredible restaurants for lunch and the two would strategically play a game of guessing, and then writing down what ingredients were in each course. Their daughters spent three days a week at the day-care center together, and the mothers tag-teamed on the dropoff and pickup.

Annette confided to Blake at one point that she'd been able to afford her luxury car with the money she'd won in a lawsuit against her previous employers. Again, Blake had a fleeting thought about the specifics of the lawsuit when she'd asked, but didn't think much more about it.

Several months into the friendship Annette invited Blake to her birthday brunch. She wanted to introduce her to all her friends and family a few suburbs away. Blake showed up at the lavish brunch where she learned a little more about Annette. She overheard a few women talking about the "career" Annette had made out of suing people. Blake's stomach dropped when she heard this, as she began putting the pieces of Annette's life together, which previously hadn't made sense. Blake clearly struggled with the great times she was having with her buddy, and the red flags that were appearing more and more frequently. She decided to ask Annette on the car ride home from the party. "So have you been in any other legal disputes besides the one with your previous employers?"

"Why?" Annette responded. "You think I'm going to sue you for some reason?"

"No, I was just curious."

"Annette laughed loud and said, 'Well, Blake, when you are wronged in this country there are ways to get payback, so, yes I have been involved in other lawsuits.'"

"Soon after her party, I decided I would try to slow things down with Annette. Too many strange and disconcerting things had happened, and I was feeling anxious and uncomfortable. I decided not to return her phone call one day, when normally I would have spoken to her several times. She called three more times that day, and as I listened to her voice on my machine, it came to me that it was not going to be so simple.

"Later that evening Annette showed up at my house. She didn't knock; I just heard the front door swing open. She headed toward my kitchen carrying a Gourmet to Go dinner for the two of us. I remember thinking as I watched her saunter with her daughter through my kitchen, 'I will never, *ever* be able to get out of this friendship.' She was slamming around, getting plates and silverware. I just sat there watching her, watching her anger brew, and wondering what I should do. It was in that specific moment that I went from seeing her as my kind, fun friend, to wondering who the heck she really was.

"I told her I'd already eaten, she angrily wrapped the dinner and put it on the counter, and then headed into the playroom where my daughter was. She put her bag down on the floor and was frantically digging for something. Finally she pulled out a lollipop and handed it to my daughter. She was talking in a loud strange voice as she packed her bag up and readied to leave. There might be stuff here I'm forgetting, but by this point every part of my intuition was screaming that this woman was off. And frankly I was getting nervous."

Blake stopped talking for a second and looked at me, hesitated, and then said, "I'm sure you haven't heard this kind of story before." As she said it, I got the feeling she was asking me . . . *had* I heard this kind of story before? And so I told her, in fact I had. I reminded her that it's not a crime to grow to know someone and then learn she's not someone you want in your life. It usually takes a long time to know all of someone. It was clear that Annette had some great qualities that anyone might seek in a friend. Blake told me, "A person just knows when something is wrong, though," and I agreed completely. All of us have experiences where we look back and think, "Why didn't I see that?"

I reminded Blake of the many women with whom I'd spoken about friendship, and the tons of different reasons I'd heard for two women becoming friends. We all need and want different things in our lives, at different times. Maybe Blake had needed Annette in her life at that time.

"Well, you can imagine that I felt trapped in the friendship big time by this point. With all the signs and questions I'd accumulated along the way, I was truly at a loss as to what to do. I've had a few friendships disappear in my life. And I've been on both sides. I'm not unfamiliar with the slowing down of phone calls, or suddenly becoming really busy. But it was obvious she wasn't going to let me *fade* her out of my life.

"After she left my house that night, I went into the play-room and my daughter was sucking on something; the lollipop was on the floor. I stuck my finger in her mouth and pulled out a large green and red capsule . . . a pill. I started to freak out, knowing there were no pills of that sort in our house. I couldn't imagine where she'd gotten it. I rinsed out her mouth and then looked at the capsule; it hadn't been broken or bitten. I looked all around the playroom but didn't find any more. I asked my daughter where she'd found it and she pointed to the floor. An hour later Annette called and asked me had I found a pill anywhere in my house. I was speechless. When I finally answered, yes I'd found a pill in my daughter's *mouth,* she responded, 'Is it still intact?' 'Intact?' I asked her, and she said, 'Yeah, is it in one piece?' I shouted at her, 'What is this pill, Annette? What the hell is this pill?'

" 'It's something I use to calm myself down, Blake. *You* need to relax.' I told her I had to tend to my daughter and that her pill was in fact not intact. I hung up on her, flushed the pill down the toilet, and started crying.

"Later that night I sat down to write Annette out of my life. I was well aware there wasn't time to ponder, because I was scared of her, in what way, I wasn't sure exactly. I decided to write her a letter and tell her straightaway that I did not want to be in her life at all, in any way. All the doubts and questions I'd had through the course of the friendship began to meld together in my mind and I was enraged at myself for not having seen earlier what looked so obvious to me in that moment, that evening.

"I wanted to stay focused on the purpose of the letter, and the purpose was to remove her from my life—period. It was tough to word it in a way that didn't sound mean or accusatory. I didn't want to hurt her; mostly I didn't want to make her mad. I tried to stay honest and direct. I told her there was no possible way that I would ever be willing to discuss or negotiate what I was about to write. I did not bring up the things she had done and said to infuriate me, because I thought it might make her reactive. And, further, it wouldn't help me achieve my goal. Instead I told her all the ways I had admired her, and the things I had learned from her. I was somehow able to articulate the great things about her, even that evening.

"And then I carefully segued into the fact that I felt she and I were intrinsically different people with different sensibilities about life, neither one right or wrong—just different. And at the end, I stated again that because of the huge differences between us, I could not have her in my life. I wished her well and signed my name.

"It was a bold move for me, Liz. A part of me was petrified at what her response might be. Before that night, I'd wished that I could act clearly and decisively in moments of panic. I'd hate to think it took my daughter almost swallowing a drug for me to whip myself in shape and do what I needed to do."

I couldn't help but ask Blake if she had seen Annette taking pills. Was she on medication? Blake told me no, she had seen her taking what Annette had told her were vitamins, and she took them often.

"When I was writing the letter," said Blake, "I was positive I was doing the right thing. I didn't need to talk about it or show it to anyone. I finished it, sealed it, walked around the corner to Annette's house that same evening, and dropped it in her mailbox."

Blake waited anxiously the next day, ready for whatever volatile response Annette might have, hoping the letter would be the end. Days and then weeks passed.

"She never came and burned my house down, and I'll forever suffer guilt that the thought even crossed my mind. I never received a letter or a phone call. More days and weeks passed, and that was it." Annette was out of Blake's life.

Months later, Blake ran into Annette's husband, who was cold to her. After an awkward moment, he told Blake that the letter and the ending of their friendship had hurt his wife more than Blake would ever know. Blake told me she hated knowing she'd hurt Annette. It stung. But she had been forthright and honest, and that, I reminded her, is what she needed to hang on to about this experience. As Oscar Wilde said so well, "The pure and simple truth is rarely pure and never simple."

Blake successfully and gracefully ended her friendship with a woman she felt was not good for her. She faced the truth as she felt it within herself and accomplished what she had set out to do. Her purpose in her letter was clear and she didn't get caught up in accusing or criticizing.

I was convinced that, executed properly, a letter was in fact a step up from avoidance as a way to end things. Having heard Grace's and Blake's and other stories I was much more clear about how best to approach writing a friend to close a relationship. If I really wanted to get someone out of my life, if I were past the need to vent and criticize in order to put things right as we can in a friendship that has a future, I could follow the format Blake had used: stick hard to your objective, which is getting the woman out of your life as quickly and cleanly as possible. The letter would not accuse or blame, but merely try to get across most effectively that you were different kinds of people. Stay away from noting any unpleasant past experiences. If you write about negative experiences and opinions that have gotten you to the place of wanting to end it, you can expect a rebuttal or response of some kind.

A well-thought-out letter is less likely to make the recipient react to it, and more likely to cause her to accept the situation.

The solution, however, will always depend on the friendship or level of acquaintanceship. Ending a friendship is really a process, and even a letter announces just one phase of the passing. Yet you have more power and room to move in by acknowledging the ending in some way than you have in avoidance.

CHAPTER FIVE

The Receiver:

Getting Control over the Unending

"What has been once so interwoven cannot be raveled nor the gift ungiven."

—MAY SARTON

S ometimes you have to make peace within yourself over an unending—that is, an ending that comes out of nowhere and has no explanation. No matter how hard you try to find out what went wrong, some women who initiate endings are not going to explain themselves.

Women who were going through a breakup with a girlfriend *as* they shared it with me have something different going on than women who recount an experience from their past.

Robin is an incredibly talented and successful artist in her midthirties whose sculpture sells in galleries all over the world. Robin and her friend Sophia had known each other six years, and had been living in the same building for the last four. An art collector and horse breeder, Sophia was Robin's greatest fan. They had what Robin described as a real, fantastic friendship. Yet Robin told me, "Sophia is done with me, and I have no idea why. We had a brief, but I thought totally benign, tiff about something stupid that involved our kids, and the next thing I knew, she started avoiding me, my calls, my knocks, and my walkie-talkie." They'd had the same set of walkie-talkies in both their kitchens for two years. Living one floor from Robin in a brownstone apartment, Sophia had decided the talkies would be perfect . . . and they were. Robin continued. "Like a five-year-old, I softly speak into the talkie at least once a day, 'Soph, can you read me? Soph . . . ' She has obviously turned it off permanently.

"For a month I've been having minor panic attacks as I step out my door to get on the elevator in my building, for fear I have to face Sophia. I feel like a schmuck. I've tried everything. Calling, e-mailing, knocking on her door, but she refuses to speak with me. I did finally see her one day, and I made her look at me. I told her this was preposterous, that I wanted to know what was happening. I pathetically apologized for anything I might have done, and basically she said thanks, and that was it. My husband is so tired of my sadness. He told me the other day he is being affected as well. In the garage every morning he sees Sophia's husband, who now doesn't say hello and snubs *him.* "Is this insane to you? My husband is being snubbed by association."

Robin's emotions were so raw that it was tough for me to even listen to her sadness. And I wanted to know what would happen in the end. When I asked her, she said, "What *is* the end? What defines it exactly?" *That* question is precisely what makes the whole experience so difficult. It's usually not clear to the one who has been dumped. Eventually Robin may have to decide that it is over for her, too, let go, and move on.

To give her some perspective, I asked Robin to try to look back on her own past and see if she could remember at any point in her life ending a friendship by "ditching out the back door," as she had so often referred to what Sophia was doing to her.

A couple of months after our conversation, I called Robin and learned that Sophia had *not* made contact. Robin had thought a lot about the question I'd asked her, and had come to find that she *had* indeed ditched a few friends in her past. She sounded shaken by her realization, but at the same time stronger.

She told me she had decided just a few days before I called to let go of the idea of a friendship with Sophia, in order to move on from the rejection and uncertainty she felt. She told me she actually had to pick the day, write it down, and feel it all day. She used it to mark the closure she'd never had, and it worked for her. She was free from the turmoil she'd felt surrounding the entire experience, because she made the choice within herself. She also told me that the greatness of their past friendship would always live inside her; it was a part of who she was now.

Not long after hearing Robin's experience, I found myself in the *middle* of two women going through what looked to be the ending of their friendship. It was the first opportunity I'd had to hear both sides, and their story falls into what I by now had found to be the most common category of friendships ended—two women who have been friends longer than three years, their contact is daily, and they describe each other as either one of their best friends or their single closest friend. More than half the stories I learned of share these circumstances. Perhaps this example can show us some alternative choices we can make.

Mia and Terry speak several times a week, sometimes daily, and see each other numerous times during the week. They are on a volunteer board together and their teenagers are both serious dance students who share the same teacher.

Mia is a casual acquaintance of mine. We live in the same community and share common interests. I was standing in front of our public library one afternoon when she approached me and asked to tell me her story, although she didn't use her friend's name.

Mia and her friend had been close for more than four years. Out of nowhere, her friend stopped returning phone calls, canceled several routine dates, and declined many invitations. Distraught and confused, Mia finally asked the woman if there were anything wrong, more specifically if she were upset or angry about something. Her friend emphatically answered, "No, nothing, not at all." Meanwhile, the two friends who had been speaking daily on the phone, and spending time together every week, hadn't communicated *at all* in two weeks.

Mia, visibly shaken, told me how the last two weeks had felt. She wanted to know what she had done to hurt her friend to the point of ending the friendship. And then she shared with me many of the things about this woman she'd enjoyed so much over the years.

Mia is the "classic" receiver in this experience. She was describing a calculated recipe for the quiet departure out of a friendship. Dr. Jan Yager, a sociologist, friendship expert and author of *When Friendship Hurts*, states, "For some, admitting to a broken friendship has become like admitting to a failed marriage. Over the last two decades, a myth of lifelong friendship has emerged, even as the ideal of a lifelong marriage has, sadly, become an unrealistic reality for many people."

"If what you've told me is what's been happening," I told Mia, "it sounds like your friend wants to get out of this friendship." She hung her head and said, "I don't get it. I keep telling myself she'll call. I keep wanting to believe, what she told me when I asked her if something was wrong . . . she told me *nothing* was wrong. When will I know for a fact we're not friends anymore? Is there a time frame to this nightmare? I can't think of anything that was strained between us recently. Maybe she's just sick of me."

We both sat there a moment and after some thought, I offered, "Maybe you should write her a letter, Mia. In it, you could sort out what you feel, tell her your confusion. You could even apologize for that which you have no idea you've done if you want. Thank her for the great times you've just described to me. It would force her to acknowledge what she is doing here, and at the same time help you to find your way to some closure in it."

"Maybe I will." I left Mia sitting at the table in the library that afternoon, and thought about her the rest of the day.

It appears that very few women can just move through the end of a friendship, without a struggle. Most appear to need to consciously put together a game plan to recover from the breakup and help them to move on. Terry Miller Shannon, a journalist, writes in an article titled "Friends Forever?": "If you're not the one ending the friendship, it feels like an elephant stomped your heart into a billion bleeding pieces."

That evening I received an e-mail from Mia telling me how much better she felt after our conversation. She said she'd begun working on the letter and was feeling some relief.

The next day I was standing in almost the same spot as the day before, because my daughter was using the library entrance to sell Girl Scout cookies, when a woman named Terry approached me. She is low key and private. I know her only casually, through the neighborhood and community.

"Liz, I finally got a moment to read your Web site. I had no idea it was all about ended friendships." My immediate thought when she approached was the fact that Terry and *Mia* were good friends . . . really good friends, always together, looking snappy and happy. My stomach dropped as the image came to mind.

Terry leaned close to me and said in a hushed tone, "I'm

going through this with someone right now. I'm trying to end it, and it's so uncomfortable." Could I have fallen into a situation where I was going to hear both sides independently?

"Really?" I said.

"Yeah, every time I see her it is uncomfortable. It's bad."

"Well, what happened?"

She was very careful with this answer. "I don't know. It's a lot of things. I just want to move on, that's all. And I don't get why it has to be so difficult. I just want to get on with my life."

"It's tough, Terry. Maybe you should talk to her and tell her what's going on."

"No, I don't want to do that," she said. "I don't want the drama, and I really don't want to hurt her. I'd just like it to be over. The whole thing feels ridiculous. The tension when I see her, it's like I'm twelve years old." Terry's manner was easy and cavalier.

"Did your friend ask you at all if something was going on, if you might be upset or anything?"

"She did, and I told her no, there was nothing wrong, because honestly I *don't* want to hurt her. I can't tell her why and all that." Yet of course Terry was hurting her friend, whom I was now sure was Mia.

"Liz, this is normal friendship stuff. Really, it's life, people move on and grow apart and change. I don't want to be friends with her, is that so terrible? I don't want to hurt her, but women go through these things. I am not a mean person, you know that. Life is short, I don't have time for drama." And then she left.

In her book *Connecting: The Enduring Power of Female Friendship,* Sandy Sheehy says, "Merely acknowledging that we might want to stop being friends with someone brings a nagging sense of failure and guilt."

I didn't detect the guilt in Terry, quite frankly, but I think that like many women who initiate this experience, Terry has a feeling of entitlement that says we're allowed to choose our friends and end our friendships in whatever way we see fit. It is our own choice and it doesn't make us bad people. All of which is entirely true. We aren't bad people because we want to end a friendship, but the way in which we choose to end it can be more or less bad in the hurt that it causes.

The contrast between Mia's and Terry's feelings is striking. For Mia, the ending came out of nowhere, throwing her into complete emotional turmoil. Terry, on the other hand, is merely annoyed by the inconvenience this experience has brought to her daily life.

Perhaps the people who are ending the friendship (the initiators) are scared they will be perceived as unkind. Perhaps what Sheehy says is right on—by acknowledging *to their friend* that they don't want to be friends, they bring on a feeling of failure and guilt. Thus they don't do it!

The receiver here, Mia, suffers more than rejection and sadness. She actually begins to question and blame herself for the failure. She puts herself through the ringer searching for answers she can never find. When all else fails, she decides to ask her friend, "Is something wrong?"

The initiator responds, "Nothing is wrong." Now the receiver can't trust her own intuition, which is usually founded on fact. The friend who is without a doubt leaving her life, has *said*, "Nothing is wrong." The initiator is *refusing* to acknowledge her own behavior, so the receiver is permeated with a sense of helplessness, because her intuition has been sabotaged. Yet instincts are rarely wrong, and it's crucial for receivers to follow them.

Writing a letter can help at this point. When Mia wrote to Terry, she got her feelings in order and down on paper, which helped her find some emotional footing again. It may have let Terry see that Mia *is* aware of what Terry is doing. Mia gains back some sense of control and can begin to trust herself again. Terry doesn't have to respond to the letter; the fact that Mia sent it was enough to give Mia the fortitude to move forward. It would also help ease her future contact with Terry, make it less fraught with emotion. Thinking of the number of times she would see Terry in the weeks and years to come had been overwhelming and forced her need to do something.

After writing a letter, the receiver can take charge and move ahead in her own life. Yet there is no doubt that a woman will mourn the loss of an intimate girlfriend just as she would mourn the death of a loved one. As shattering as it is, how we choose to handle it can become a profound lesson in resilience.

Most of the women who decide to end a friendship have been toying with the idea well before they actually start leaving, so by the time they do begin their quiet departure, they are already emotionally detached. That's very evident in Terry's side of the story. I've yet to meet an initiator who had any idea of the total emotional upheaval she was causing in her friend's life. In fact, her intent is to avoid hurting the friend she's leaving. Initiators believe at the time that they're doing the right thing. In fact, they feel consciously decent and kind, as they think they are saving their friend from the crushing reality. Initiators are so emotionally detached that they don't see their friend is already suffering.

To choose to avoid rather than confront is tempting. Because there will be no outside judgment it becomes even more tempting. Then we convince ourselves we do it to spare the feelings of our friend, who will surely be hurt by the truth about why we don't want to hang out with her anymore. To the initiator of the ending, it can feel almost too good to be true, and a lot of the time it is.

We have to consider the consequences of our choices. Our not acknowledging that we are indeed ending the friendship is what could be considered lying by omission. To deny something is wrong when a friend asks, is an actual lie.

An alternative for Terry's "Nothing's wrong" is to acknowledge to Mia what is going on. It is tougher to think about than to actually do it, but once it's over, it's really over. By not addressing the problem, she guarantees discomfort and unhappiness for days, weeks, and maybe years.

It is simple human nature to want to avoid conflict. Sandy Sheehy says in *Connecting,* "The idea of ending a friendship is something women kind of chicken out at." It's their desire to avoid conflict, or their wish to be seen as "nice."

Those who initiate the ending don't really want to hear advice. As a former serial initiator, I know this from experience. Once this process gets going, it is very difficult to switch course. So initiators should give conscious thought to an ending *before* actually starting the process. Friendships define so much of who we are, they deserve our acknowledgment of their endings. These girlfriends we've loved have had a huge effect on our lives and we on theirs. We need to pay attention.

CHAPTER SIX

The Initiator:
Taking Control of the Ending

While writing this book, I got a panicked message on my machine one day from my friend Rachel asking that I call her back as soon as possible. When I reached her later, she explained that she was going through a rough time with her friend Ann. She'd spent the last two days sifting through her feelings and getting them down in a letter. She asked if I would read this letter and share my thoughts, which I was happy to do.

These two women had been very close friends for more than fifteen years. They spoke numerous times a day, saw each other weekly, and relied on each other for emotional support. Their sons, born minutes apart, had also become great friends. Rachel is a remarkable woman, whom I call my very own "Martha Stewart." She astounds me and all her friends with her limitless knowledge of food, crafts, and entertainment finesse. Her creative gifts, cakes, breads, and children's activities belong on an infomercial. Without my asking, Rachel arrives at my doorstep a week before my annual Christmas party bearing handmade, intricately beautiful holiday wreaths and decorations. She offers to drive my family of five to the Los Angeles airport during the holiday season . . . and means it. She is a giver and all who know her appreciate this.

Rachel had slowed down a lot of the normal activity she usually shared with Ann. She hadn't wanted to spend much time with Ann, and felt taken for granted and unappreciated lately. She figured that having some space would give her time to figure out what to do. I could hear the enormous resentment and regret Rachel felt in her voice. Ann's behavior and Rachel's disappointment in her friendship were definitely taking their toll.

Rachel was much more emotional and vocal about a letter that Ann's son had sent to her own son, which contained some very hurtful accusations that Rachel found inappropriate, than she was about Ann's overt behavior toward her. Rachel felt the child's letter was Ann's idea and filled with Ann's thoughts. She was outraged that Ann would choose the twelve-year-old as the messenger for her own judgments and insecurities. Rachel did not give the letter to her son and decided to deal with the situation by writing her own letter to Ann.

Rachel's experience particularly interested me because she and Ann had been friends for such a long time. Most of the letter-writing between girlfriends at this point in my research had transpired between friends who'd only known each other a short period of time.

Rachel sent me the letter she had drafted but seemed to be falling into the trap of venting and accusing Ann in her single spaced, three and a half pages. I called her up and asked, "Rach, what do you want?"

She answered, "What do you mean?"

"Well, have you thought about exactly what it is you're trying to accomplish with this letter? Do you want to end the friendship?"

Rachel was silent a long time before replying. "That's a good question. I hadn't really thought about it that way. I think I'm done. I mean, I'm willing to be done. She doesn't give back, Liz, she just takes."

She was right according to what I'd read: a list of all that Ann had done to piss off Rachel. In response to all the invitations and great efforts that Rachel had made over the years, Ann seemed to have reciprocated almost nil.

I said, "Rachel, you spend a lot of time pointing your finger at her here. You're telling her all the things she didn't do, and all the things you did do, which, believe me, she already knows. I'm thinking she's going to have a tough time hearing what you're trying to say if you go at her this way. Do you really *want* her to hear you?"

She didn't hesitate and answered, "Yeah, I do." I couldn't help thinking that as much as Ann had taken and taken, Rachel had also given and given without ever saying anything or stopping until now. And Rachel admitted that she was disappointed in herself for not having addressed these problems earlier.

"Okay," I said, "so maybe you could try to go at her with the same information in a different way. If it were me, I would simply state how her behavior made me feel, as opposed to telling her what her behavior was. I might even add that I should never have allowed this behavior to become acceptable in the friendship. I would get specific about what it is you would want in a healthy, reciprocal friendship. Not that you shouldn't vent, but in venting you might want to stay focused on the subject, which is for her to hear you. And to leave the door open for the friendship to continue."

Rachel sat with this for a moment and then said, "I get it and you're right. You're really right."

"Okay," I said. "So for instance, she knows, Rach, all the times you've had them over and all the efforts you've made. She *so* knows. Maybe instead of listing all that, you could just say something like, you can count on one hand the number of times you feel she's reciprocated."

Rachel laughed out loud and said, "Maybe deep inside I want to hurt her, the way she's hurt me. I want her to know all the crap I've put up with because of her. I'm kidding, of course." I laughed a little with her, but wondered how much truth there actually was in that statement. I felt protective of Rachel and her generous heart, but I didn't know both sides of this relationship, so I tried to keep my own judgments and opinions quiet . . . and listen.

We moved on to the part of the letter that made no sense to me, in which Rachel talked about their sons, commenting on Ann's parenting and the difference in the ways they deal with their sons. I asked Rachel if her letter were meant to address *both* her and Ann's relationship *and* that of their sons. She answered no. She intended to address the friendship between the mothers, period. She said she had put all the kids stuff in because Ann always has been obsessed with the friendship between their boys. Rachel was sure Ann would try to use the boys to stay in continuing contact, or to buffer or avoid differences between the two of them.

So we came up with a very specific beginning, which we hoped would clear any questions about why Ann was writing the letter.

Dear Ann,

The intention of this letter is to distance myself from this friendship for as much time as I need to figure out what I want to do. I understand that in making this decision, I must address the boys. Having given it a lot of thought, I am comfortable with the idea that my son take some time away from your son. This was a difficult letter to write in that we have such a long history together, but you must understand that the contents of this letter outweighed and won against that history.

I try hard in my friendships to be happy for the people I care about in my life, for their accomplishments, their other friends and all that makes their life content. I so often feel you struggle with this part of our friendship. I even feel sometimes you don't want me to have other friends at all, which puts me in a very difficult, sometimes impossible position.

This is not the way I want the friendships in my life to run. If your son's letter to my son was some kind of attempt to see us more, or make things better I'm sorry to say it totally backfired on you. Ann, it is so important that you understand, this is not something I am willing to discuss right now, it is simply me saying I cannot and don't know when I will be able to be in a friendship with you and these are the reasons.

Rachel was elated with the result and sent it by e-mail. I told her that very few people could receive a letter such as this, and *not* respond to it. I expected that Ann would contact her, whether by phone, letter, or even coming over in person.

Not three hours later, I picked up the phone and heard, "You're never going to believe this." Rachel's voice had the familiar sound it takes on after about a glass and half of some good red wine. She'd received a response from Ann by e-mail, a three-page single-spaced response.

I sat and listened to the whole thing. Ann's letter opened and continued for an entire page on the subject of the boys, which is exactly what Rachel had anticipated. Rachel's letter had that one statement, which was meant to address the boys but led Ann to the point of the letter, which was to address *their* friendship. Even I was frustrated, as a simple bystander, with Ann's obvious ability—or determination—to miss that point.

The first part of the letter was overly dramatic on the subject of Ann's son. She told Rachel that the entire family, particularly her son, would have to suffer the consequences of Rachel's harsh decision. Ann said she would have to explain to her son that his best friend's mother has decided to force the ending of the kids' friendship, and the letter her son had written intended for his friend had been confiscated. Rachel's letter had not said the friendship between the kids was over, but that Rachel was willing to allow her son to take some "time away."

Rachel became more and more upset as she continued reading the lambasting of herself as a parent in Ann's words for another full, single-spaced page. I had to stop her. "Rachel, I cannot believe she didn't get it, she didn't get for a second, that this was about your friendship with her."

She answered, "I know, now I'm the lunatic bitch from hell who cares nothing for the children."

"Okay, go on." I said. A page and a half later, Ann finally commented on the friendship between the two of them.

She explained that as much as she appreciated and enjoyed Rachel's hosting everything, she was also well aware that Rachel was a total social control freak. And on numerous occasions when trying to reciprocate, she had realized Rachel simply wanted to do it all. Ann explained her behavior as graciously stepping back and allowing her friend to do what made her happy. She felt that Rachel obviously gauged a good friendship on how many invitations were extended, and that she, Ann saw friendship as more of a spiritual exchange of support and "being there" for each other.

Ann's letter abruptly ended with her not being able to believe that Rachel was wishing her well, when she was purposefully and clearly hurting Ann's entire family.

Rachel was sobbing after she finished reading this to me, feeling terrible guilt for being honest and hurting this woman and her family.

"Liz, maybe I shouldn't have sent her the letter. I mean, I don't want to cause pain to people. She said I hurt her more than anyone's ever hurt her."

I listened to Rachel and then I said, "Rach, I'm not a shrink, but one thing I know for sure is this is a time in your life that you have stood up for yourself and your feelings. You gripe all the time about how people take advantage of you, how you're too nice and you don't know how to say no. This was a good thing you did. Ann doesn't know the new you, she is addressing the old you, and you have to find it in yourself to be strong and stay true to *yourself*."

Rachel had begun seeing a therapist just weeks before she had decided to write this letter, and together they had decided that Rachel needed to start taking charge of her life. She wanted to stop worrying about people being mad at her. She wanted to stop her constant impulse and need to rescue and aid others. She wanted to begin believing, she had told me, that there's room to say no and still be a good person.

Rachel had made a brave choice with her letter. Her therapist had warned her that changing behavior is never easy. Old habits die with great difficulty, I thought as I watched Rachel grapple with choosing between what she wanted to do and what was familiar. I hung up the phone, drained from the conversation.

The next day Rachel called me on the way home from

her therapist, sounding strong and back on track. After reading both letters, Rachel's therapist told her she felt that the two women were so far apart on so many issues, she couldn't imagine the friendship ever finding a common, reasonable place.

But when Rachel returned home that day, Ann's twin sister, Caroline, was sitting at her front door. Rachel said her heart dropped as she stood up to greet her.

"Listen, Rachel, this is ridiculous. You and Ann have been friends such a long time. Ann is so upset and my nephew is beside himself at the prospect of not spending holidays here at your house this year. They've never missed a Passover together." Passover was four days away, and Rachel didn't know what to say to her.

Caroline leaned toward Rachel and said, "Some bad things were said in anger with the swapping of letters, Rachel. Maybe if you just call Ann and apologize we can put this behind us."

Rachel said nothing. Caroline walked to her car, and before she opened the door she turned toward Rachel and said, with no sense of humor, "Now, don't make me come back here."

I wanted to drop-kick this woman, at her nerve and condescension. Passover came and went. Rachel told me a few weeks later that Ann had called. They spoke briefly about the letters and the situation, and it was strained and awkward. Then Ann suggested the families get together for dinner. Rachel reluctantly agreed but at the same time told Ann she wasn't willing to move anywhere in the friendship the way it had been going. She basically set up the boundaries and even gave warning that she would be calling Ann on her behavior as she saw it. They met a week later for dinner.

Rachel described it as uncomfortable but something she knew she wanted to do. And Rachel was okay with how it transpired. As my mother used to say, "The greatest lessons in life cannot be taught, but must be lived."

Only a couple months have passed since all this happened. Rachel has received a few calls from Ann, but hasn't seen her again.

I asked Rachel to be totally honest, did she have any regrets about having written the letter? She answered, "No, I don't regret a word of it. I needed to do it. The letter was one of the best things I've done for myself in years. I can't help thinking of my life a year from now without having ever addressed this. That thought assures me I've done the right thing." She paused for a second and then said, "In a way it was sad and a little bit terrifying to face the reality of my friendship with her. I'm so used to packing it all away and not dealing. That was the terrifying part. And the sad part was having to look at the reality of the friendship and where it had landed. There's a part of me that misses what it used to be with Ann. We had such a great thing going for a long time. I think, no, I *know* the friendship will never be what it was. I want to say there is something really freeing in being able to say and live all of this out loud, you know?"

Living through Rachel's story was emotional, exhausting, and cathartic for me, too. After having heard dozens and dozens of stories, I now can guess pretty accurately the general history of the friendship and the trajectory it's on within a few sentences of a story. But Rachel's story was unique. She not only chose to communicate through a letter, she continued a relationship with her friend. Ann had been a lost girl in the making—a loss stopped by the fact that Rachel had addressed, acknowledged, and moved their relationship to a different place.

Rachel and Ann got me thinking about my own past experiences. Rachel had been very clear about what she didn't want in the friendship from Ann. She also stayed surprisingly open to what the end result might become. She was *willing*, she said, to have it be over. Never did she say it *had* to be over or it *had* to stay intact. Indeed, she herself was changing.

What had been *my* reasons for leaving friendships and not addressing them? When I had initiated the ending of a friendship and had contemplated acknowledging the ending with my friend, I had feared it would lead to a discussion, which could very well have led to a compromise or settlement, as with Rachel and Ann. But when I had initiated an ending in the past, I had been unwilling to have those friends in my life in *any* way. I had not wanted to compromise. At the time I had felt that no matter what they said or did, we would not continue the friendship and nothing would have made me want to stay in it. I hadn't wanted the possibility for reparation, pacts, promises, or space. I had wanted out.

I kept thinking of my friend Maggie, who had dropped me so hard. As I watched Rachel struggle to be straightforward and set up boundaries, and even admit her resentment, I kept thinking that no matter what her friend Ann thought at the time, it would ultimately be far better than getting the silent treatment and forever trying to guess what the hell had happened to make her lose Rachel's friendship.

Many women who had *initiated* endings to friendships gave me the standard reasons of "we'd grown apart" and "she changed." These women consistently seemed to bail on their friends . . . leave them and not tell them. And most of them described themselves as having been in the friendship for a long time.

Melanie told me about a long-term friend from college, whom she'd been thinking about removing from her life for a good three years before she finally did it. In her mind, her friend had become superficial and materialistic; her values had changed from when they were younger. This friend had come to represent almost all the qualities Melanie doesn't generally like in *any* woman. The thought of actually sitting her friend down and telling her she wanted her out of her life nauseated her. Again and again Melanie tried to prepare some sort of departure, but each time she found herself filled with guilt and fear. Eventually, she was so frustrated and angry that she was able to completely drop her friend. Melanie stopped calling and responding to calls completely, and avoided all contact. She vanished from her friend's life without a word. Yet she describes it as, "Something I try not to think about, but I struggle with it."

In contrast, another woman told me that she had never given a second thought to dropping her friends without a word of acknowledgment. She told me her life was too short and busy to bother with the trivial things in life that could "bring her down." She told me she had recently ended a friendship made on her first job, a friend with whom she had been close for ten years. They'd had a misunderstanding regarding a lunch plan, and she decided she was finished with the relationship. After ignoring and avoiding several of her friend's phone calls and visits, she defined the friendship as over, and professed to have no other thoughts about it. As insensitive as it sounds, in an odd way it reminded me somewhat of where I had been in my life before I decided to write this book. Although hopefully I was never as seemingly self-absorbed, this woman and I had shared a familiar sort of denial. But I had gotten past my refusal to look at what these experiences had done to my friends—and me.

I think that ultimately this woman is going to feel *something* about these abrupt, heartless endings. My personal experience would indicate that an onslaught of emotions would eventually creep up on her.

Other, more common reasons for ending friendships that I heard were, "She's crazy" or "She bugs me." The "crazy" answer almost always came from women who'd known their friends for a fairly short period of time, rarely more than two years. The "bugging me" answer, on the other hand, seemed to come repeatedly from women who had been in the friendship for many years.

Jillian seemed particularly flippant about suddenly ending a friendship of twelve years. Jillian and her friend Kate had known each other for eight years when they both decided to move out to Los Angeles from Philadelphia. Two struggling actresses, they were doing all they could to survive in Hollywood. They handed out movie passes, worked at coffee houses, and sold Tupperware. But mostly they were each other's lifelines during what Jillian described as the most difficult time in their lives. They pooled their money and enrolled in an acting class, which Jillian assured Kate would change their lives.

In fact, four years later, Kate got a huge break and was booked for a television show that became a hit. As Jillian told the story of her friend's success, her face changed a little and she looked up at me and said, "That's when she really started bugging me."

I asked, "You mean her success bugged you?"

"Yeah, her success bugged me. And how it happened, and what a fluke it was, and what really bugged me was she didn't care about it nearly as much as I did. *I* was the actress among us. She was still sort of figuring out what she wanted to do. And then, well, then that was it. I just walked out of her life and never said a word."

"Why did you feel you couldn't tell her your reason for wanting out of the friendship?"

"I didn't feel the need to tell her at the time, and basically she was just bugging me. She bugged the crap out of me in every way. From how she always had to be right, to the loud smacking noise she made when she chewed her food." Her answer was something you might hear from an old married couple, which I told her.

Her response was, "No, because when you marry someone, you think about the fact that it will be for life, you make a vow, and know you have to live through the things that bug you, but when it's a friendship, there's an option."

And I answered, "Isn't that the truth? There's an option, there are quite a few options." I asked Jillian if she ever considered the fact that Kate, whom she'd known for all those years, might still be wondering what devastating thing she must have done to merit that cold and abrupt ending.

She pondered that and said, "No, I think she knows, I really do. She'd become so annoying, she *had* to know." Jillian seemed to feel very little remorse or responsibility, but after we talked more she became more contemplative, as though she'd never *really* thought about how her friend might feel until that very moment.

What she'd shared with me was a far cry from, "I ended the friendship because of the way she chewed her food, and because she acted like she knew everything." *This* was specific. Jillian was so envious of her friend's success, she simply couldn't be around her. And she seemed to agree that she had never given that reason a conscious thought until the moment she talked with me.

And then Jillian told me just how difficult it had been for her on the inside to have to come clean with her story. We talked about the beauty and the curse of denial. She told me this experience was just about the ugliest thing she'd ever revealed about herself to anyone.

She said, "The idea that I would actually walk away from the greatest person in my life, because I couldn't find it in me to be happy for her, makes my skin crawl."

I think Jillian found comfort in knowing she wasn't the only person in the world to make a decision about a friend that she later regretted. And we both decided that people just do what they have to do, and then later one hopes that they grow and learn.

Jillian and I became friends after this conversation. I asked her if she'd seen Kate since the ending. She answered,

"No, not in real life." But she'd watched her religiously each week on the show she'd been doing for six years.

After Jillian left that day, I pulled out an old *People* magazine from the bottom drawer of my desk that I'd gotten about five years earlier. There was a picture of my friend Maggie, whom I spoke about at the very beginning of this book, in the top left corner. I'd seen it on the stands about six months after she'd disappeared from my life.

The caption read, "Star tells all about the struggles of life."

The magazine reported that Maggie had gone public with numerous personal problems with which she had been struggling for years. It was like reading about someone I didn't know, yet these things had obviously been going on all through our friendship. I felt stupid and naive and sad and pissed all at the same time. But mostly I felt terrible that Maggie had lived with all of this inside for the entire time I knew her. As *I* sat in the friendship feeling totally connected, she was suffering.

Maybe, too, I felt a tinge of morbid relief from the article that her internal hell might be to blame for the sudden death of our friendship. After I'd read the article for the first time, I'd shoved it back in that drawer, never told anyone I'd seen it, and never discussed it with a single soul. A few people had mentioned over the years hearing things about Maggie, but I'd just smile and say, "I don't know."

Yet seeing the magazine and learning of her struggles was worse than having been left to guess forever. It made me see that I, who pride myself so greatly on my ability to read and care for people, had obviously failed her more miserably than I had ever guessed, and that was sad.

I met a woman named Reese through a friend of a friend. We started talking and she told me she wanted out of her friendship with a close friend named Colette, and was slowly fading herself out of their everyday life. Reese said she had many different reasons for wanting to get out of this eight-year friendship, but like most, she was vague about specifics. I also felt she was being somewhat defensive, so I tried to remain a sounding board for her rather than offering my own perspective.

Reese was clear that she still cared for Colette, but at the same time was ready to move on. Now that Reese had made up her mind, she didn't like the uncomfortable feelings her avoidance brought when the two would see each other. Reese's own theory of why female friendships end is that endings are a natural process, a part of personal growth, and though difficult, they're necessary for each person's development.

While I can agree with this to some extent, I believe that a growth in consciousness would also require the acknowledgment of what was happening, and I felt I had to tell Reese as much.

"What do you mean?" she asked me when I finished.

"Well, I think you make a great point, but how can anyone grow or move if we don't acknowledge the situation and address it with one another? You know a lot of women in your friend's position feel really hurt by this kind of ending."

"No offense, Liz, but why make a production out of

something that is so simple? I think women tend to get too dramatic with each other. I am trying to keep this clean."

Reese was becoming irritated with me. I don't consider acknowledgment drama, but clearly she did and she didn't like looking at what was happening in her own life from another perspective. I didn't want to push her, so I said, "Let me know how it goes, Reese."

A week later I saw her at an art gallery and after a while meandered over to her. Immediately I felt the same slight irritation in her that I'd felt the week earlier. I tried to keep it light, and I was *not* going to ask about her friend.

"How are you, Reese?"

"Good." She was hesitant for a moment and then she said, "Not so good, actually. In fact the friend I was telling you about last week is here. I don't know how it happened. She was supposed to be out of town. It's stressful. Just the mere fact that she is in this room is stressful to me."

"Why?" I asked.

"I don't exactly know. I mean I feel bad when I see her. So I'd rather not see her." Reese seemed not only stressed but also angry.

"Well, she'll get over it, Reese," I told her, and then she excused herself and greeted some women she knew. I walked around for a while, trying to figure out who Reese's friend was as I scanned the room, but couldn't. I waved to Reese an hour later and left.

Several days passed. I was talking to a friend in front of the yoga joint near my house when I saw Reese. She surprised me by politely interrupting my conversation and asking quite seriously if she could speak with me alone. Honest to God, I thought she was going to yell at me, because I had gotten the feeling in our last two conversations that she thought I was trying to challenge her.

"Liz, I wanted to tell you something. I need to tell you something. Remember when you said, that the way I was fading out of Colette's life hurts a lot of people?"

"I remember."

"Well, I thought about it, and I was sick thinking that I might be hurting Colette. So I thought about it a little more and came to see that my problem with her doesn't require that she be out of my life *completely*. I somehow thought I had to weed her out altogether, but I don't.

"See, here's the real deal," said Reese. "Colette is a one-on-one type of person. She doesn't ever hang in groups and likes to keep very private. I've always had a lot of friends; I'm really social. And since we've been friends I don't really see anyone else. I love Colette, I think I was just feeling smothered by her. She was taking up so much of my time, I felt like I couldn't have other friends in my life. I realize now, I can, I just have to let her in on this, and we'll figure it out. I never wanted to not be friends with her, but I got angry and reactive. Fifty-three years old feeling self-conscious in front of my friend talking to other friends, it was very disconcerting.

"I think, Liz, that when you're in this situation, it's hard to step back and get perspective . . . really hard. And I'm sure, had I not had those conversations with you I wouldn't have come to this on my own. It was the thought of Colette hurting that got me to stop and try to figure this out. When I decided to avoid her, it's like I had blinders on. When you're in it, you can't see much." Then Reese thanked me. She even hugged me.

Many of us who decide to initiate the ending of a friendship tend to "lock" ourselves into an absolute position on it. It's a big and daunting deal to decide to exit from someone's life, no matter what has happened or what we tell ourselves at the time. Some initiators feel trapped by their circumstances as though their only option is to end the friendship completely. So, because they can't see other possibilities, they use this locked-in position to help them follow through with what they're sure will be difficult, but is right for them at the time. Yet it can be very hurtful and even counterproductive for you to lock up and not even consider another option. Most friendships can withstand some change. You don't have to make the choice of being friends in a certain way, or not being friends at all. Rachel and Ann, Reese and Colette, took the time to learn how they could change things to be better for both parties. They knew that in fact they *did* want to remain in each other's lives, but they needed to address some issues in order to do it. I think most of us could benefit from stepping back to get a better perspective on what is happening and force ourselves to look more carefully at what we want and how we can get it. Maybe we all also need a nudge now and then to remind us that everything great takes work. About true friendship Mother Teresa said this: "To keep a lamp burning, we have to keep putting oil in it."

CHAPTER SEVEN

The Irony of Confronting:

Can This Friendship Be Saved?

"Resolve and thou art free."

—HENRY WADSWORTH LONGFELLOW

As I thought about the many stories I'd heard about women ending friendships, I realized that they were all laced with the common thread of avoidance. I couldn't help wondering if we women were avoiding confrontation in general or just confrontation in our female friendships.

For me, confrontation in *any* area of my life does not come easily. In fact, whenever humanly possible I choose to flee rather than face the conflict. Though I do find a way to rise to the occasional challenge when inevitable, my overall knee-jerk reaction is to find a way around it. But after hearing the stories of women who faced up to the need to end troubling acquaintances and put old friendships on a new, different footing, I felt inspired to challenge myself. Maybe I'd gleaned some inspiration from Grace and her courageous confrontations with her mother and Shay. Under the influence of these straightforward women, I decided to confront an acquaintance named Hilda, someone whom I'd met seven years ago, who had resurfaced in my life and was causing some unpleasantness.

When I had met this woman at my daughter's ballet school, I was in an unfamiliar new-mother, new-path time in my life. Another young mother, she was nice enough, but she had a manner that ultimately didn't appeal to me. I saw her several times a week at the school, went to a few dinners at her home with other women from the school, met her at a beach club once with our kids, and that was about it. A few months after we met, she began calling and inviting me to join her for this or that function; I always politely declined. Yet her calls became more and more frequent. I continued to decline and tell her how busy I was, but she just kept calling. Shoot me, but I didn't want to be her friend. I didn't get a good vibe, and I didn't want to hang out with her. She was clearly not getting my message, and the more I made myself unavailable, the more she pursued me. She extended invitations to everything from dancing at nightclubs to bowling. I just kept saying no thank you, but eventually I stopped returning her phone calls.

Several days passed before I received a message from Hilda that said, "Hi. Listen, I've called you five times in three days, and unless you've been mugged and had the five fingers on both of your hands chopped off, I expect a simple call back."

Who would say that to someone? Was that supposed to be funny? To me it was completely creepy, and the few close friends I told were in total agreement.

In retrospect this was a perfect opportunity for an easy confrontation. After that message I could have called to tell her that I didn't have the time right now in my life for another friend and I hope she would understand. But I didn't, and from that time forward, my avoidance of her became intentional, whereas before I had felt a little guilty. She had just wanted to be my friend, and I had felt a little bad that I couldn't reciprocate. But now in my mind she was plastered with a big red WARNING sign. From then on I greeted her at the school but cut myself off from any situation in which we'd have to talk. She was obviously angry with me and started talking badly about me to the other women. Not long after the disconcerting message, however, I learned that she was moving and her daughter would be leaving the dance school. I endured her mostly passive but sometimes actively unpleasant behavior toward me for a short while longer and then she was gone.

This could have been a fairly benign, easily forgotten experience, but four *years* afterward, I showed up at the first day of kindergarten for my daughter. I'd fallen in love with this particular school, and done everything possible to get my daughter accepted. In a crowded, competitive city like

Los Angeles, it's truly on hope and a prayer that any parent gets her child into her school of choice, but something good was going on somewhere, and she got in.

Our entire family proudly walked my daughter to school in her pressed plaid uniform and spanking-white school shoes. We arrived and were given red name tags to wear, a code system for the teacher to whom the students were assigned. We were told to look for other families with red name tags and introduce ourselves. After about forty-five seconds I saw another red name tag—pinned to the shirt of Hilda, the woman who had left me the weird phone message. She was talking with another red name tag. I couldn't believe it. Of all the schools, of all the people, of all the luck.

I thought that four years was a very long time and that she would be over it. She would have lived so much life she would barely remember she ever knew me, and I'd had two more children by that time. So I decided to approach her rather than wait. Covering my trepidation, I greeted her with a big smile, hoping she could be a grown-up and we could begin anew. But she was totally cold and rude, so rude that the few mothers standing around her became visibly uncomfortable. I must have made a great first impression— I hadn't been at my daughter's new school *five* minutes and I already have one enemy and three strangers wondering who I could be, and what I could have done to deserve such malice from a fellow mother.

This woman was a genuine annoyance whom I could definitely have lived without, but our children were in the same class, and assuming no one was moving, they'd be in the same grade for the next twelve years. As I saw it, there was only one choice for me. Rise above it, be kind, and move on. However, for her, four years seemed to have fueled a major resentment and dislike that she took no pains to conceal. That first year she ignored me, gave some icy looks, and snubbed me. But mostly she became unnerved whenever I arrived on the scene and would leave my presence, as though she might catch whatever I was carrying that repelled her so much.

I have to say, it was beginning to piss me off. Our first year at that school was such a great experience except for the unpleasantness I'd come to expect from Hilda. So the next year I decided it was time to face my challenge. Hilda continued her regular behavior toward me, sometimes a cold hello, most of the time blatant snubbing.

Every year, the school hosts a coffee for the mothers in each grade. I was late arriving and slipped in unnoticed. I scanned the room for friends and caught Hilda scowling in my direction. I smiled and waved her way. She turned around and fled.

Later that day, driving in the car, I started to think about why and how this woman could be so unhappy with me. Was it really that I didn't want to be friends with her four years ago, or did she just think I was a horrible person. I wanted to know, I wanted to define it, I wanted her to own it so we could clear the air and move on.

I got home, looked up her number, and dialed. I felt like a third-grader, my heart pounding, my hands sweating.

She answered the phone and I said, "Hi, this is Liz Pryor."

She hesitated and answered, "Oh, hi." I tried to ignore the effort she put into sounding as unthrilled as possible.

"Well," I began, "I've been meaning to call you for quite some time. I need to ask you a question."

"What is it?" she said.

"Well, have I done something to offend you or make you mad? 'Cause if I have, I am unaware of it and would really like to get it straightened out."

"Why would you say that?" she asked.

"Well, because of the way you treat me. You are cold and rebuffing, as though something is bothering you." My nervousness had vanished and I started thinking this was a really good idea.

I waited for her reply. I was ready for anything, for her to launch into: "Four years ago," or "Our kids . . ." Anything. And then she said, "My husband's been out of town lately and I feel like I'm so distracted, the September 11 anniversary came up and well, I guess I've been thinking about it a lot." She just started babbling, I mean really babbling. I almost didn't know how to respond, but wanted to say, "Yeah, yeah, yeah, but why are you such a bitch to me?"

After yessing her for a while I interrupted. "But is there anything I have done or said that you can share so we can try and move beyond this?" She then began new babble about her kids, nothing even remotely connected to my inquiry.

When she finished, it sounded as though she was about to try and get off the phone. Before that could happen I said, "Well, then, I guess I've mistaken all this unkind behavior."

I waited and she mumbled something I think was, "I guess so."

I waited again, and then asked, "Am I crazy? You're not going to admit you've acted unkindly to me?"

"Life is hard," she responded.

I then said, "Okay, I'm trying here, I really am, and I'm not getting anywhere. Can I expect the next time we see each other, and all the times that follow, your behavior toward me will be civil?"

She answered, "Yeah, I guess so."

"Great," I said, and before I could feel anything she'd hung up.

So there it was, the big confrontation, which had been pretty anticlimactic. Even though I thought I knew her reasons for snubbing me, I had wanted to hear *her* reasons. I was willing to explain myself to her but she didn't come close to revealing her feelings or explaining her behavior.

Simply deciding to confront doesn't guarantee that you'll get answers. The receiver has to be willing to participate. Even though Hilda wasn't willing, I still got what I needed, to my surprise. She chose to bypass the reasons, which brought us straight to the behavior. After refusing to address the issue, Hilda did begin to treat me with civility, and I felt an enormous sense of relief. I had done what I could do to better the situation for myself. These types of experiences can exhaust a person emotionally. I was so sick of thinking about her, and the little ways her behavior crept under my skin. Those feelings all dissipated for me after addressing this woman. I felt empowered. In fact, I knew that if she were to begin acting badly again, I would not even care.

I don't take much credit for finding the courage to confront Hilda. She wasn't a *friend*. There were no real stakes involved. I hadn't shared my heart with her . . . she was simply someone who was bugging me. Perhaps this confirms what I had already discovered: avoidance seems most likely to occur when two women have genuinely shared a friendship, a mutual swapping of hearts and emotion. Ironically, the norm for ending women's friendships seems to be, if we care deeply, avoid; if we don't care at all, confront!

This particular confrontation got me thinking of other confrontations I'd had, almost all of them with men. The breakups with all my old boyfriends were lined up in perfect little packages, stored on an old dark shelf inside me. Yet I hadn't even installed a shelf to mark the end of my friendships with women.

I got to thinking about one relationship in particular I'd had, well before I met my husband, Thomas. I was living with my boyfriend, Rick. We'd been together a couple of years when I slowly realized that I wasn't in love with him anymore. I don't know what happened. I was madly in love with him when we met, that desperate, had-to-be with-him-every-second kind of in love. I was crazy in love for months, talking about baby names and dream homes and growing old together, all the stuff that would make it utter torture to leave someone. When the revelation of wanting to leave him sank in, I fought desperately against it. I prayed every night that I would somehow wake up in love with him again. Didn't happen.

I couldn't imagine how I could sit down and tell him I needed to leave, to move on and look for the love of my life. He was a good man, and I was sick at the thought of hurting him. I'd broken up with many guys in my life and it had always been awful. So I stayed with him much longer than I should have, avoiding the inevitable. I became a miserable wreck.

I called my mom one day, so frustrated and wracked with guilt, sobbing and snorting and falling apart. When I finished a very long, dramatic version of the situation, she paused and asked dead seriously, "Well, do you think you should marry him because you feel sorry for him?"

That question stopped me for a second as I thought about its absurdity. "Mom, don't be ridiculous. No, for God's sake, I can't marry him."

"You said you wanted to marry him last Christmas, honey. Are you sure you don't want to?"

"Mom, are you not hearing me? I definitely am not marrying him, I don't love him, I have to leave, I have to move out of here, and he's just going to die."

"Is he really, honey? Do you actually think he's going to die?"

"Maybe, Mom . . . maybe he will."

"Let me promise you something, honey. No one in the history of the world has ever died from love, okay?"

"Michelle Pfeiffer did in *Dangerous Liaisons*," I shot back.

"Well, this guy is certainly not Michelle, sweetheart. There is no way around this. Hang up and start packing."

I remember thinking how much I hated having to be responsible. I wanted to run away from having to face the truth as I knew it. It just sucked. I had two choices at that juncture. My mom was right: marry him because I felt sorry for him, or tell him I was leaving.

It was brutal when it happened; I was inches from caving when I saw him weeping and begging me to stay. He told me he could change, he would change, I could find the old love.

He didn't die, but I almost did, of guilt. Matter of fact, anyone in my life at that time probably wanted to kill herself listening to my miserable self-torture, until the day I asked Cara to come with me to pick up the TV I'd left at the apartment in my hurry to get out.

It had only been a month since I'd moved out, and I simply could not face his sadness alone. I needed Cara to come to the apartment with me in case he got emotional at the sight of me. I was afraid he could go crazy, maybe force me back in the apartment. Cara agreed and we drove over there. We both stood at my old front door like trick-or-treaters waiting for it to open. Finally the door opened and there appeared before us a very cute blond woman wearing my old robe.

She looked at us strangely and said, "Can I help you?" Cara and I must have looked like twins, with our dropped jaws.

"Yeah," Cara suddenly sounded like a bouncer from New York. "She needs her TV," pointing to me. The brokenhearted boyfriend came up and stood behind Blondie. He was shuffling a bit and staring at the floor. Cara shoved past them and headed for the television, which was on and in its place inside the hutch he and I had gotten at a flea market together.

She yanked the plug out, hoisted it, and shoved past them again. I'm not sure I ever closed my mouth through the entire exchange.

My adrenaline was soaring as we lugged the TV to my car. We didn't say a word to each other while we secured it in the back.

"Asshole," Cara said as I started the car.

"Total asshole," I said. And then I cried.

That breakup was clear, compact, and final. The confrontation was something I clearly struggled with, but I did it. After all my whining and stressing, I eventually faced up and broke off the relationship—because that is what you do. That is the protocol when it comes to male-female relationships. After the confrontation, there was never any second-guessing, speculation, or confusion about what happened and what the future would hold. So what is it exactly about friendship with women and relationships with men that carry such different agendas at the end?

While researching her book *Connecting*, Sandy Sheehy consulted more than thirty different psychologists and sociologists. I was most intrigued with what she'd learned about society's influence on female friendship. She writes that friendship is a surprisingly "loose" and "fuzzy" term in the eyes of philosophers and psychologists. Unlike most other relationships, "Friendship lacks sanctions set forth by society to describe its responsibilities." Perhaps that helps explain why the endings are so often irresponsibly and haphazardly executed. Friendship lacks definition in its structure and its bonds. It is described by the experts as one of the very few voluntary relationships that exists, making it more easily prone to rupture.

Although women's nonmarital relationships with men don't have formal definitions or rules either, choosing a boyfriend is voluntary. Yet, regular good old-fashioned boyfriend-girlfriend relationships usually merit a full acknowledgment and confrontation at their finish.

Ella, from Detroit, told me of a confrontation she had with her friend Jill when they were in their late twenties. Different in almost every way, they had met as young children. Ella was outgoing and athletic, a social animal whom people seemed to naturally gravitate toward. On the other hand, Jill was an introverted, wiry intellectual whose idea of the perfect day was to be locked in her apartment reading a book.

Ella said that when they were little kids, Jill would sit fully clothed beneath an old black umbrella at the beach and read, while Ella, in her checkered bikini, would build a sand stage right next to her, decorate it with shells and driftwood, and then stand up and sing her lungs out into a sand shovel microphone. When Ella was reading *Little Women,* Jill was discovering Tolstoy. Through puberty, dating, first loves, college, and marriage, these two women remained important friends to each other. Their history, Ella told me, had always kept them connected.

Ella made another friend named Trish soon after she was married. The two had a lot in common. A true extrovert and a veterinarian, Trish was also a marathon runner, which Ella, who also loved animals, had recently become. After a tough ten months of training and then running the New York Marathon together, they became very close.

After several years, they decided to pool their ideas and

love for animals, and together opened an animal rescue mission, a dream come true for both of them.

Although Trish and Jill had met on a few occasions, Ella explained that the friendships never crossed over. The dynamics with each were such that Ella kept their friendships in separate compartments of her life. A few times Trish had asked if there was something wrong with Jill because she acted as if she didn't care for Trish, but Ella explained that Jill was just a bit temperamental, and was sure it was nothing personal.

Soon after the animal shelter was up and running Ella found out she was pregnant with her first child. Both of her close friends were excited for her. Jill soon made plans for a baby shower and Ella asked Jill, early on, to make sure she included Trish in the organizing and planning of the shower. She told Jill that Trish would never want to impose, but at the same time really wanted to help. Jill called Trish to get the shower plans in motion, at which time they swapped catering names and other ideas. Trish also told Jill her idea for a surprise song she was putting together for Ella and the baby, which would include the barking of both her and Ella's dogs together. Ultimately, they all decided to have the party at Ella's house because it was perfect for the occasion.

Fifteen women filtered into Ella's backyard on the day of the shower. Jill was busy greeting guests, when Ella noticed Trish looking a little down. The standard games, food, and mimosas soon came to an end, and as Ella was opening the last gifts, Trish stood up and made a heartfelt toast. She mentioned her lifelong dream of the rescue mission, and how it became a reality. She finished by playing a CD of the song she'd put together with their two dogs barking. The shower guests howled with laughter, and gave it a standing ovation. Somewhere in the commotion afterward, Ella overheard Jill make a cutting remark about the CD to Trish, who, Ella noticed, remained very quiet. Moments later, Ella again noticed Jill saying something rude to Ella. Ella had described Jill as quiet and reserved. Ella knew she could get caustic with people, but she had never seen her come close to treating anyone that way . . . ever. Knowing Trish the way she did, she became concerned that if Jill had been treating Trish unkindly—perhaps even all the way through the shower plans—Trish would never have said anything because that's just the way Trish was. Ella's surprise and concern was turning into anger.

After she was clear that Jill had been behaving unkindly and inappropriately toward Trish, Ella took a few moments to figure out how to handle this. After she noticed yet another exchange in which Jill was downright rude to Trish, Ella knew she would have to say something to Jill.

Throughout their friendship, Ella had never raised her voice or had anything more than a short argument with Jill. In fact the only other *women* she'd ever confronted as she knew she had to confront Jill—with her blood boiling and heart pounding—were her mother and one of her sisters. As the guests continued chatting and looking at gifts, Ella grabbed Jill by the hand and led her into her bedroom. She shut the door and locked it.

"What the hell are you doing, Jill? What is wrong with

you?" she said. Shocked, Jill laughed uncomfortably and said, "What are you talking about?"

"Are you sick or just nuts? What is your problem with Trish? She has been nothing but kind to you, and helpful, and great to me, would you agree?" Jill stood there, almost frozen. Ella continued. "You have been so rude to her." Jill remained frozen for another moment, and then finally responded.

"You are not treating me like a best friend, Ella . . . at all. You're ignoring me. You've made no special gestures of thanks to me. I feel ripped off here. *I* am your best friend." Ella was floored by the shocking reasons for Jill's behavior, but shot back, "This . . . Jill, today, the shower for this huge belly, these gifts . . . this is about *me,* not you."

"Yeah, well, you need to act like the best friend you're supposed to be," Jill said.

"You will no longer *be* my best friend, Jill, if this is how you behave. I am going to walk out of this room and try to forget that this sophomoric, selfish bullshit happened on the day of my baby shower. If you can't figure out a way to grow up and get with the program, be nice to people, and get over yourself, then leave . . . just leave. And apologize to Trish before you go."

Jill walked straight out of Ella's house that day and they've not spoken since. It had been almost a year. Ella seemed lost in thought after sharing the story. I finally said, "Is it a pride thing, do you think?"

She answered, "Maybe it was, in the beginning. I felt she should call and apologize for her behavior that day, and maybe she thought I should call to apologize for losing it on her. I don't know. The baby is here and I've been wrapped up in this new life. And I think it's terrible she didn't call after the baby came."

"Do you miss her?" I asked.

"Of course I do . . ."

"But not enough to call her?" Ella thought for a moment, and then she said, "I don't know. The days turned into more days, and then into weeks . . . And no time ever quite felt like the right time, if I had to be the one to make the gesture toward reconciling."

Ella has only a few regrets about how she handled that day with Jill. She felt strongly about what had gone on, but she wishes she had controlled her temper. She wishes they could have discussed Jill's obvious pain about their friendship, and the wedge Jill felt Trish had put between them. I was baffled, however, that an argument, even such a heated argument, could lead so quickly to the death of a friendship so rich with history.

History is simply not always enough to hold a friendship together. Jill and Ella had grown apart, but because of the bonds of their childhood, they had a hard time noticing. Any problems that came up were easier to dismiss, because they'd known each other so long.

Confrontation doesn't necessarily lead to the resolution we want or expect. In fact, Ella's confrontation led to a different kind of avoidance. Ella and Jill are not filled with questions about why their friendship ended, yet Ella feels anxious, as if their future is in limbo. She has no idea what will happen, but hopes they will find a way to reconcile. At present, she can't imagine her life indefinitely without Jill as a part of it. Perhaps their argument indicated that they needed to make a shift of sorts in the friendship.

Another story came my way from Page, a truly extraordinary woman in numerous ways. She found herself at a crossroads in a friendship with her dear friend Deandra. Their relationship occupied huge chunks of her memories, from childhood on. All of the glimmers of good times Page remembered as a child had Deandra in the picture with her. Both women had come from tough, challenging backgrounds. As small kids they had lived in a low-income housing project on the outskirts of Chicago, and had fought like dogs to weather together what Page described as "times that feel like a lifetime ago." Deandra had faced an unusual amount of tragedy in her young life, having lost both parents and her only brother. Page believed that the glue that held their friendship together for so long had formed as they got through those sad and difficult times. Together they had successfully climbed out of poverty, gotten educations, and begun promising new lives.

Little by little, after finishing college, however, Page felt the connection with her friend slipping away, as if the friendship were surviving on history alone. Holidays and birthdays, anything celebratory, Page and Deandra habitually spent together, as Page was as close to family as Deandra had. Well after she was married and her children were born, Page felt the need to move out of the friendship with Deandra, as they had developed intrinsically different attitudes about their past and present and life in general. But Page felt guilt and empathy for Deandra's past tragedies and even guilt over her own satisfying life and family, because Deandra had not found someone to love. This outweighed Page's genuine desire to leave the friendship.

But Page did begin to cut back on the times they visited and the amount they spoke, in hopes of creating the distance she needed. But for several years she didn't dare cease contact altogether.

On the brink of ending the friendship by increasingly avoiding Deandra, Page said a miracle occurred. Her friend Deandra's life took a sudden turn and she fell in love. For the first time, she loved somebody, and he loved her back. Page saw Deandra's sudden state of contentment as her cue to leave. Deandra's happiness became the catalyst for Page's departure from her friend's life. But instead of sliding out and avoiding Deandra, Page decided to write a letter of departure. She couldn't think of a better time to follow the truth of her own heart and end the friendship, honestly. And so she wrote:

Dear Deandra,

I can't tell you how happy I am for you that your life has finally found the stride you have searched so hard to find.

Please believe me when I say it is difficult for me to write this letter. We have climbed mountains together, and I know I would never have made it, if not for the strength I got from you. I will always be grateful to you, and I will never forget our past together.

We have both changed so much over the years, and our

differences have gotten in the way of my feeling that we are good friends for each other.

I must acknowledge this need in myself. It is time for me to go, Deandra, to leave this friendship. I didn't want to slip away and disappear, as I know it could never have gone unnoticed for both of us. I realized I wanted to do the right thing, and feel strongly that this letter is just that. In order to honor our friendship I needed to tell you the truth. No guessing, no guilt. You may not see right now why or how I can feel this way—I can only hope that you accept it as the truth, which is all I know to give you. For any of the anger or sadness this letter may cause you, I am sorry.

I wish you happiness, grace, and peace in your life— always.

Page

Page's recipe for resolution and peace was ultimately quite simple. She went with the truth and acknowledged her friend, the care they had given each other over the years, and the need to end their friendship kindly and lovingly. A few weeks after Page sent the letter, Deandra called her. She quietly told Page how saddened she was that their life together was over, and then she wept her thanks for Page's honesty. Page told me that, as sad as it was, there was resignation in Deandra's voice. And they both understood that this resignation defined the ending of their relationship for both of them right there in that very moment. The friendship had been so big for both of them, and that was honored in its ending.

———

Confrontation doesn't necessarily lead to resolution. In fact it can lead to places you never even considered. Within romantic relationships it is effective, and usually results in finality. On the other hand, Ella's confrontation has so far led to alienation, sadness, and uncertainty. But Page's more measured approach brought not only ending but an emotional closure for both. Confrontation can bring movement, but for a good resolution, perhaps we need a clear intention.

CHAPTER EIGHT

The Etiquette of the Ending:

To Lie or Not to Lie

I n my constant search for guidelines and advice about
women's friendships, I started listening to Dr. Laura
Schlessinger, the radio talk show host. I wanted to hear
how this expert would advise a woman going through a
friendship ending. Pulling into my driveway one day, I
finally heard the call I'd been waiting for.

Dr. Laura announced, "A female caller waiting on the line
has a question about how to end a friendship."

A woman in her twenties had called in. She was ready to end a friendship with a woman she'd known since they were ten. She described a few things that had come to bother her about her friend, and then added that they had been slowly growing apart. Yet she was sure her friend did not feel the same way, and was very concerned that the ending of this friendship would devastate her. This caller had already decided to end the friendship; her question was how she should do it. This is how I recall Dr. Laura conducting the call.

Dr. Laura asked her how she *thought* she should do it, and the woman responded that she really didn't want to hurt her friend's feelings, but felt it would most likely require a conversation letting her know it was over. The doctor replied, "Good."

The caller then said, "But I *could* just stop contact, you know. Wait till she got the message and move on, right? I mean if I really am going to end it, she doesn't need to hear the reasons why, which I *know* will hurt her, does she?"

Dr. Laura paused and asked her, among other things: "Have you begun trying to let her know in other ways?"

"Yes, I've already stopped returning calls, I stopped the spin class I took with her. She knows something is up."

After a long pause, the radio host offered, "Well, I don't think it's necessary to go into the details of why, but a true sit-down telling her you've grown apart might be necessary in order for closure."

I have to say I was surprised and impressed that Dr. Laura would give such a nuanced answer. Perhaps this subject is even gray to people who usually see in black and white.

My friend Rooney had also been listening in for a friend-ship call on Dr. Laura's show, so as soon as the call finished, my home phone rang. Rooney had majored in psychology and obtained a master's in sociology before joining the ranks of television producing. She now wanted me to meet an old friend with whom she'd gone to school, Dr. Susan, a practicing psychologist with a specialty in counseling women. I called her, and arranged to meet for lunch.

She was sitting at the table when I arrived, nicely dressed, much younger and hipper than I'd imagined. We greeted and after a few moments, I could see Dr. Susan was not only sharp, she also had a great sense of humor. I took advantage of an opening at the end of a funny story about Rooney and decided to get to my subject.

I explained that I'd become interested in the topic of women and friendship, specifically how women end friend-ships with each other. I shared my own story and how I had excavated my ended friendships. I touched on the guilt and shame I feel around it all. Dr. Susan agreed with my belief that society and people in general overlook the significance that the loss of a friend can have on a woman's life.

Then I asked her, "What advice might you give a client if she came in seeking help during a fallout with a friend?"

She looked down, moved her water glass around, and said, "I'd tell her to try and be as direct as possible."

I added, "But to do what feels right for her?"

"Yes, something like that."

"And what about the woman on the receiving end of this, the one who is basically getting dumped. What would you tell her?" I asked.

"She usually doesn't have as many choices. I would remind her she is only in control of herself and then suggest she ask her friend why she seems so unavailable."

I then asked, "Even demand it if she has to?"

"Right." She smiled.

I took a few seconds and then asked, "And what if this happens to you? What do you do?"

"Oh, my God," she said, and took a sip of water. "Well, nowhere near what I advise, unfortunately." She fussed around with the silverware and then said, "It's ironic actually, but *I* have a situation going on as we speak, with a friend from graduate school. It's been long in coming, but it's here. I'm avoiding, I haven't returned calls, all of it. I'm really unsettled about it." I couldn't help wondering, was the friend a shrink also?

She continued. "This is a very murky situation for me. I mean, obviously I need to give this subject in my own life some serious thought."

I asked her, "Have you considered your own advice in terms of dealing with your friend?"

She responded, "No, that wouldn't exactly work for me." I wanted to tell her it doesn't exactly work for anyone, as she continued.

"If I really think about it, I guess what most women want from me when they present this situation in my office is permission. Permission to feel and to do whatever they want, and I must admit, I usually give it to them."

"Are *you* looking for permission?" I asked.

"Maybe, but I already know that however I decide to end this friendship, I am free from judgment. I only have myself to answer to."

We ordered our food, and then she asked me what *I* thought she should do.

I said, "I can't answer that. I mean, I don't know you nearly well enough to answer that."

She displayed her savvy therapist side and offered, "Okay, then I'll rephrase the question to make it so you can. What would you do if you were me?"

I thought about it and then blurted, "I *was* you many times over, and when we were just talking about permission it made me realize that it's actually permission that helps navigate the course we choose to take at an ending. The tricky part is that the permission needs to come from *ourselves*. It's not going to come from the outside, from our mothers, or society or whomever. I mean, it would help, I'm sure, if the world around us would force an expectation of behavior, but they don't, not in this area. So we have to do it alone. And that is a tall, tall order for some of us. As I'm sure you've seen, even with no threat of judgment from the outside, women still grapple with whether or not they're doing the right thing, and *that* is coming from inside of them.

"What I've learned is that there is something in all of us, like a moral barometer of sorts, that helps keep us who we want to be. Maybe it's made up of all we know and have learned about right and wrong and good and bad. It is in fact, the gauge by which a person can feel that her own behavior is acceptable or unacceptable to herself. I think it's where random pangs of guilt and maybe those emotional gray days come from.

"Maybe there is no blanket advice when you're talking

about something as variable as this. Everyone has her own barometer based on who she is and where she came from. It took more than ten of these endings for my own moral barometer to explode. I was forced by all that makes me who I am to turn around and take a closer look. And the result, I hope, is that I am now closer to living where I can feel better about who I am."

I finished by saying, "You, of all people, must have a gauge on how different this moral barometer can be from person to person. I mean, it's not murder or child abuse we're talking about. It's the fine moral line in all of us that dictates how we treat ourselves and others. Am I ranting?"

"No, not at all. I love it," she said.

So I continued. "I was pretty horrified to learn that over the years, I had gradually strayed so far from the standards inside me. This is the best advice I can give, as old-fashioned and clichéd as it may sound. It's simply a matter of looking inside yourself to find what works for you. Which, by the way, could very well be avoidance. Women do it effectively every day. The only catch is the aftermath."

Dr. Susan said, "Well, I already know that avoiding is causing too much of a stir in *my* barometer. It's an honesty thing for me. It just feels dishonest for me not to somehow acknowledge it, and that's probably more due to how I was raised than the fact that I am a therapist. I really don't want to confront her and list my reasons. So, what now?"

I'd thought about this as we were talking, so I said, "Well, I think I can help you write a heck of a letter. . . . You could simply tell her you feel the friendship is over, give her a general idea of the ways you've grown apart, thank her for her time in your life, and that's it. Clean, honest, and it carries closure." I shared a range of the letters I'd read or heard about—and their aftermaths—and we came up with one she felt would work well. We exchanged numbers and she offered to help with further questions I might have.

So there it was. I had *finally* gotten a couple of hours face-to-face with an expert, but ended up discussing a friendship *she* was in the process of avoiding. I think the fact that Dr. Susan is a therapist may well have had something to do with how easily she came to find she couldn't avoid her friend. Her comment on honesty really hit a chord. Suddenly, it was clear to me that my own lack of honesty through those endings had created a significant part of my angst.

Standing in line at the market a few days later, I grabbed a few magazines to flip through in carpool. One blurb attracted my attention:

TIME-SAVING TIPS
How to Get Off the Phone Fast

Contrary to popular belief, you can short-circuit a friend without causing offense. Here's how.

- At the office and don't want to talk? Say, "My boss is standing at the door. I have to give him a report."
- At home anytime between 5 and 9 p.m., say, "I'm just sitting down to eat."
- If a really gabby friend calls, ring the doorbell for

> authenticity and say, "Sorry I've got to go, someone is
> at my door."

The list went on, and the idea was clear: if you want to get off the phone fast, *lie*. I looked for the author of the "lie list" and found that the tips were taken from a recently published book on etiquette. *Etiquette?*

Are we actually a society where an average female reader can come upon something like this, take it as authority, without raising an eyebrow, and read on? I hope not. Something is just not right there. Not that I don't support sparing people's feelings. Call me crazy, but what about the good old-fashioned truth? *This is a bad time, can I call you back?* Ring the doorbell for *authenticity?*

I looked up the definition of etiquette in the American Heritage dictionary: "The practices and forms prescribed by social convention or authority."

So do random people in society take it upon themselves to try to instill conventions such as blatant lying?

I simmered down when I found a review from a well-known *New York Times* book reviewer on the book from which the lies were taken. He railed against the idea of lies and lists of nice behavior being misconstrued as etiquette. As he nicely put it, "Good society has clear rules, because, otherwise it would be *bad* society." He revealed that the author of this book on etiquette had suggested the reader not look at etiquette as a daunting set of uptight rules to follow and pointed out that, "Rules are *supposed* to 'daunt' as they would be useless if they were otherwise low, loose, and whatever the opposite of uptight is." This reviewer's comment that rules make society a "good one" really stuck with me. The endings of friendship between women have yet to merit acknowledgment, let alone rules, within our society. But perhaps the seemingly useless advice doled out so consistently by the experts is an attempt at creating something for us to try to follow. The avoidance so commonly used to end things has led quite clearly to lying. Whether by choice, omission, white lie, or conscious deception, lying has become part of the process.

I remember the first time I ever questioned the technicalities of lying. I was in third grade and I had arrived at school one morning to find that my best friend, Carolyn, had chopped her signature long hair into a short above-the-ears pixie. She looked nothing like the friend I'd known and loved for three straight years. I was horrified.

As I slowly made my way into our house after school that day, I found my mother sitting at the kitchen table with my little twin sisters. Distraught and upset, I announced to her the news that Carolyn had cut her hair to her ears. My mom took a second, smiled, and then asked why I should care so much about the length of Carolyn's hair.

I told her it was horrible, and she looked so different, and then I mustered up the courage to say out loud what I'd been thinking all day, "She looks like a boy, Mom!"

"Does Carolyn like her hair, honey?" she asked.

"Yeah, she loves it."

"So what's the problem? That's all that matters." I had

already lied and told Carolyn I liked it, because it was so awful I didn't know what else to say. I didn't want to hurt her feelings, as I quietly confessed to my mom.

My mother calmly explained to me that I had done nothing wrong. I was baffled. The queen of the Roman Catholics was okaying a lie. She sat me down and explained this no-fault lie rule. If you lie to hurt someone, get yourself out of trouble, or make yourself look good, it was wrong and bad. However, if you told a "little" lie to spare a person's feelings, it was okay. It was a different thing. It was acceptable.

I returned to this concept again and again that evening. Finally, my mother became frustrated with my inability to just live with the new information, and escalated from talking to shouting at me. "She can't do anything about the hair, honey. She can't *tape* it back on. What good would it do to tell her?" I decided to bring the subject to my true WASP of a father to get another perspective. Dad was huge on etiquette and protocol, manners and appearances. We were seven of the most manner-informed children on the block.

I knocked on the door of my father's study so I could get his views on Carolyn's hair. I heard him say, "Come in," and found him sitting in the big leather chair reading a book. I hopped up on his lap and presented my case concerning Carolyn's hair.

He asked, "Do you know what a 'white lie' is?"

"Yes, it's a little lie, I think."

"Well, no, it's a little different than that." He stood up to get a very thick, worn, leather-bound copy of the Oxford English Dictionary.

"Let's see what this says." He handled the old dictionary with great care. "Ahhhhh, see, here it is. The first citation reads, '1741 in Gentlemen's Magazine XI a certain lady of the highest quality makes a judicious distinction between a white lie and a black lie. A white lie is that which is not intended to injure any body in his fortune, interest, or reputation but only to gratify a garrulous disposition.'" Then he pulled out another reference book and read, "The actual term 'white' in 'white lie' is based on the age-old black-white dichotomy, where the former means bad and the latter good.

"I think the book is saying that sometimes, when communicating with others, it very well may be okay to express an opinion for the sake of making someone feel better."

"Soooo, sometimes it's okay to lie?" I said.

I saw the rare look of uncertainty come over my dad's face as he reluctantly offered, "Well, yes, I suppose sometimes it's okay. Sometimes in life things are not just one way or another. Often it depends upon the situation."

There I had it from both parents, each clearly perplexed in his or her own way about how to how to make sense of a significant yet ambiguous reality of life.

Splitting the hairs of lying, white lying, sparing feelings, and gauging which is which is still serious business for me. Just the other night my kids were watching the movie *Harriet the Spy* for the first time. I decided to join them. As I sat down, my daughter Conner, almost nine and the eldest, paused the movie and asked if I'd like her to fill me in on what had happened so far.

"You see," she said. "This little girl is eleven, and she only has these two friends. The rest of the class doesn't like them. There are two really mean popular girls and they tease and make the little girl feel bad. I guess she's like a misfit, Mom. Anyway, she loves writing. She writes everything down in her journal, like a diary. She writes very funny and sometimes mean things about the mean children. And her parents don't spend enough time with her, but her nanny is great and lives with her and is like her mother."

"Okay," I said. "I think I got it." She started the movie and the next scene showed the Big Boy Bully of the class stealing Misfit Little Girl's diary, and then Popular Mean Girl reading it to the entire grade while Misfit Girl stood by cringing. Everything this little girl ever thought or felt was written in this journal. Not only the mean truth of the other kids, but also the hurtful truth of her own two dearest and closest friends.

The two misfit friends, angry and hurt, then teamed up with the rest of the grade to make this one little girl's life a living hell.

Just as the entire class plotted during art to pour a gallon of brown paint over the head of the misfit, I got up, paused the movie, and said, "I don't think this is a good idea."

"Why, Mom? We know it's just a movie, it's not scary."

It was scary to me. Why expose them to the abhorrent exaggerated depiction of the cruelty of kids? I was overruled and reluctantly started it.

The nanny, this little girl's only friend in the world, was fired by the parents, leaving her totally alone. The poor girl suffers the ridicule and torment of the other kids, incapable of sharing any of her pain with her parents, who ultimately decide that perhaps bringing the nanny back might help them find out why the daughter has become so despondent.

The nanny returns and, within seconds, learns the truth of the little girl's life. They are lying in a cozy bed together just having discussed the horrible chain of events. The nanny says, "Well, sweetheart, beauty is truth and truth, beauty. That is all you know on earth and all you need to know. That's John Keats."

The little girl responds, "What does that mean?"

The nanny offers, "You're going to have to do two things here and you're not going to like either of them. You're going to have to apologize, and you're going to have to lie."

My seven-year-old son, Augie, at this point whispered under his breath, "She's telling her to lie."

The little girl in the movie then says, "But you told me never to lie."

"A little lie that makes people feel better isn't wrong. Sometimes a little lie can be a big help."

The girl in the movie thinks about this and says, "Okay."

The wise mentor of a nanny then says, "Good friends are one of life's truest blessings. Don't give them up without a fight." Following her advice, Harriet ends up back in the good graces of the friends and on great terms with her parents.

My daughter asked me at the end of this movie what I thought of the little girl's white lies to save her friendships. I stammered and stalled as my kids looked at me with those big eyes that remind me that my answers will affect their lives.

I finally said, "You know, there are so many tricky little things in life, and I think this white lie, little lie thing is one of them. I'm positive you guys understand the basics of right and wrong. I know you know the difference between a truth and a lie, so I'm going to say this. In this movie, *no*, I wouldn't have told her to lie. I would have told her to focus on the truth, which was that she was so sorry the words in her journal had hurt her friends' feelings. I would have told her to let her friends know how much she loved them and she could even say she would never again write down anything that might hurt any of them."

Augie nodded as though he knew this would be my answer and was clear. My four-year-old, Luca, kissed my forehead and Conner said, "Why *did* they tell her to lie in the movie, then?"

"Well, I suppose the nanny was saying, 'Just say you didn't mean any of the things you wrote,' so the kids would forgive her."

"Well, it's not so tricky, Mom, if you just stick with the truth then."

Right, I thought. And I was positive this wouldn't be the last conversation we would have about white lies.

What I wanted to tell my kids was that I'd asked *my* parents the same thing thirty years ago, and they had also told me a white lie could be a good thing. That I had clearly partaken in numerous white lies throughout the years that I'm sure spared many feelings. But that the fuzzy line between a white lie and a lie could bring on something not so good. Maybe they would have learned something from hearing that most of the endings to my friendships had begun with the innocence of a few white lies meant to spare a friend's feelings, and then progressed to lying by omission, which inevitably became avoidance. To not tell a person a truth, because it may hurt her, is shortsighted. To avoid contact with someone so as not to have to address the truth is a form of lying by omission, regardless of good intentions.

I wanted to tell Conner to be very careful and use the barometer I knew she already had, because by reading that barometer she would always know she was staying true to who she is. I wanted to tell her that I'd rather she not wake up in twenty years with a big dark cloud looming over her conscience, wondering where that had come from. I hoped that as she grew older she would always know how to care for her friendships in a truthful way that would leave her smiling and contented at all stages of her life.

After talking with Conner, I remembered a story I'd heard while researching this book. Born and raised in Savannah, Georgia, Lucy was an eccentric woman whose life and stories were impossible to forget. The first time I met her, I saw her large white straw hat before I actually saw *her*. She was sitting at a table in her favorite French bakery in Los Angeles, on Ventura Boulevard. She definitely looked to be more in her fifties than her true age of sixty-eight. She stood up, smiled, and hugged me as I arrived. Even though we hadn't met until then, in four seconds I felt as though I'd known her for years.

I sat down, and happily began listening to the greatest southern accent I'd ever heard. "I was my parents' only

child, you see. I'll just tell you a little bit about my background, because it might help you, right?" She took out a
white handkerchief with her initials monogrammed on the
corner and dabbed her lips before continuing.

"My parents wanted more than anything in the world for
me to have a well-rounded, wonderful life. Very near the top
of the list of most important things were manners and etiquette, right or wrong. That's what they taught me. By five
years old I knew more than most adults know about table
manners, thank-you protocol, and meeting and greeting.
My parents, bless their souls, couldn't have any other children and maybe they felt guilty, and that's why they paid so
much mind to teaching me every little thing there was to
know. I wanted to tell you my story because what I was
raised on, and I mean driven into my core, was good old-
fashioned friendship, and the value it would bring my life.
And I can swear to you, sweetheart, I've lived it and it is as
true as that hot sun beating on our heads sitting out here.

"Now I am a people person; I am still in touch with
everyone I have ever known, and that is who I am. You're
laughing now, but I mean it. When I was eight years old, my
daddy gave me a copy of the book *How to Win Friends and
Influence People.* That was my life, you see.

"So there were five of us friends. There are four of us
now, but I'll tell you that part later.

"At my very first day at The Dancing/Manners Academy,
which my parents insisted I attend, I met a girl named
Cheryl, who ended up becoming the best friend I would
ever know. We were six years old at the time. Together,
Cheryl and I met Rita at our Catholic grammar school that

same year, and by the time we were ten, we had formed our group, The Three Saritas. Pronounced of course in the worst Spanish/Georgian accent ever heard—Sar dee tahs! We'd stolen a book from Rita's older sister. Yes, we had to steal it because it was forbidden for us to even look at it. It's title was *Sarita's Love*. It was the story of a sixteen-year-old Mexican girl named Sarita who ran away from home to be with the love of her life. The three of us spent the next eight years memorizing every line of the inappropriate book, while we attended The Sacred Heart School for girls. We were at the school for twelve years, and in that time, we only initiated one more friend into the club, but we had to change the name, to The Sarita *Club*. Maryann became our new member. She was the smartest and most organized in the group. In fact, she's the most organized person I've ever known to this day.

"Upon our graduation from The Sacred Heart high school, I decided to give each of my friends a necklace with a small gold disc with *Sarita* inscribed on the back. We left for four colleges that year, and swore on our lives, and the Sarita Club, we would always stay in touch.

"Our junior year in college the four of us convinced our parents to allow us to take a boat abroad for the exchange student program in Paris.

"On the boat over to Paris, we met a woman named Mari Elena, from Mexico City. She had the smallest feet I'd ever seen on a grown woman. Mari Elena clicked with the four of us . . . from the very beginning. By the time we got to Paris, she had become our fifth Sarita.

"While in Paris that year, my friends Cheryl and Rita had

a difficult time together. We'd all lived a long time apart, and for some reason those two struggled something bad around each other. One night I remember Cheryl gasping enthusiastically the way she did, at the sight of a beautiful statue we'd seen in a museum. Rita cut her off before she could finish, and told her how full of crap she was, that everything was so beautiful and everyone was so fabulous. They drove each other crazy that year.

"When we returned to the States for the summer, Rita got a job on the other side of town and we didn't see much of her. Mari Elena had come back with us to Georgia and my parents of course invited her stay with us. They thought it might help me become more well rounded to learn Spanish. Thing of it was, Mari Elena never spoke Spanish. She and I spoke in French most of the time so my parents couldn't understand what we were saying.

"The night before Cheryl was leaving to go back to college, she got a call from Rita. I remember thinking, thank God, the two of them are going to patch this up and everything's going to be fine. But Rita apparently had a lot to say to Cheryl that wasn't so great. Cheryl wouldn't share what happened exactly, but she left that night in a very bad state. Being the busybody that I am, I went over to Rita's the next morning to try and find out what had gone on. I wanted everyone to get along, you know, that's the way I am. Rita told me she'd decided she had grown out of Cheryl, and would appreciate it if we'd stop writing and calling and behaving like schoolgirls; she didn't want to be a part of the Saritas. I tried everything I could to get her to tell me what had happened. Then I shared with her that the club was just a way to remind us of who we are to each other. She said she'd rather not remember. And that was, frankly, the end of Rita.

"Course, it was hard on all of us. Mari Elena cried for hours the night this happened, and Maryann made lists and lists of the reasons we should help them work this out. I just believed somewhere in me that this would work itself out sooner or later. Although we weren't spending as much time with each other in those days, we kept in touch constantly through letters and phone calls. The next Christmas, we all thought, and I prayed, we'd hear from Rita, but we didn't.

"And then time passed, a *lot* of time. My parents passed. Our children were married. Our bodies dropped . . . and we learned how to play bridge. Feels like it was not so long ago, and I know I sound like an old lady when I say that. But especially Paris, it feels to me like yesterday.

"Cheryl and Mari Elena and I eventually settled not so far from each other, and Maryann ended up in a suburb about an hour away. We met monthly, all of us. We've *been* meeting for I think thirty years or so. We have a serious bridge club that we don't miss for anything. Between us we've shown up with grandchildren, broken hips, shingles, postpartum depression, preteenager depression, postdivorce depression—you name it, we've gone through it.

"For a long time we spoke about Rita as though she were there, but eventually we stopped talking about her so much. Yet something always feels like it's missing without her, it really does. Being who I am, on more than one occasion I tried to find Rita . . . many times I tried, but I never had any luck.

"And then about three years ago, we all received invitations from the Students' Abroad Association for what was titled 'A ship to Paris reunion.' It had been forty years since we were on that boat, since we met Mari Elena for the first time, and we were tickled at the idea of going and seeing all those old faces.

"We wondered about Rita, but no one said anything. And then the strangest thing happened. Cheryl told us she couldn't make it to bridge, just about a week before the reunion. I of course canceled bridge that evening. Cheryl had *never* missed. She told me she just wasn't feeling well, and I knew better, she must have been downright dying not to be at my house. I headed over there, got my key out, and helped myself right in. I walked into her bedroom and there she was, looking peaked and awfully weak. Her beautiful white puffy bun of hair was down and lifeless. Her eyes looked heavy when she said to me, 'Do me a favor, Luce.'

"I answered her, 'Anything.' She smiled and asked me to sit next to her on the bed. She'd gotten out her old pictures. The both of us sat there looking at ourselves at around seven years old, dancing dresses and party shoes on, standing in front of the manners academy where we'd first met. I laughed a good laugh seeing us there so young and awkward. I said to her, 'Can you believe we were ever that young Cher? What a life, huh?' But she'd fallen asleep, so I closed the picture album and sat there for a while. Next to her bed there was an envelope that had the name Rita lightly written across the outside. I didn't dare open it, but I *was* curious.

"I left that night and decided Cheryl must have really needed a break. She had a busy life, and was always doing for everyone else. I asked my housekeeper to come with me the following morning to help, and I brought a brand-new bottle of the old-lady shampoo, as we all called it. We had discovered the shampoo in Mexico while visiting Mari Elena when we first started going gray. We all believed it when the old Mexican woman told us it would help keep the gray hairs from getting coarse, and we'd been using it for years.

"I walked into Cheryl's room that next morning and told her I had a spanking-new bottle of the old-lady shampoo for her. And there she was in the exact same spot she'd been the night before, only her face was paler and her eyes were a little bit open. I put my hand over her cold face and shut her eyes, and then I looked out the window and my heart felt broken in half.

"I sat on the bed where I'd sat just the night before. I called Mari Elena and we sat together with our friend, waiting for Maryann to arrive. Cheryl's husband had passed away many years earlier, and she'd never had children. Mari Elena walked in and noticed the envelope next to the bed with Rita's name on the front. She gently picked it up and read,

My Dear Rita,
Long good-byes are not for you, you told me that once when we were seventeen. So my friend I will say it quickly. I am sorry, I have missed you dearly. Forgive me for not having come to you sooner, and I forgive you. Please embrace your friends who love you, and know that we will all meet again as we've always said.

Sarita love,

Cheryl

"Mari Elena noticed there was a much smaller envelope near the bedside lamp. She picked it up and saw the letters M. E. on the front. 'That's me,' she said. She opened the little envelope and inside was Cheryl's gold Sarita disc necklace.

"Mari Elena cried and laughed at the same time. She had complained *forever* that she hadn't had the Sarita necklace like the rest of us. I hooked it around her neck and then the three of us wept."

I looked at Lucy and asked, "What about Rita?"

"Yes, Rita. Well, we contacted the Paris boat reunion people and they had found her. Rita was living not too far from me, and when I called she agreed to come. We had a beautiful reunion with Rita. For me, it was a dream come true. We gave her the letter, and we had a new Sarita necklace made for Cheryl to be buried in.

"We meet once a month now at Rita's. We play bridge, we're in great health, and the Sarita Club is back with all its members. We toast Cheryl at every game. You see, sweetheart, of all the things Cheryl could have felt unfinished about in her life, it was her friendship with Rita that must have felt most unsettled. There she was in her parting moment and with the chance to fix a regret. I wasn't so surprised. No matter what people tell you, when it comes time to leave this life, nothing, I mean nothing matters more than the love and ties you have with the people in your life. My parents knew it, and now I know it. In fact my daddy used to say, 'There ain't a person in the world who leaves this life wishing they'd had fewer good friends.'"

Lucy reminded me of my mother. They share a similar clarity in the choices they've made about parts of life that matter. *Unlike* Lucy, however, my mother's accent is standard American dialect with a twist of British, although she was raised in our hometown of Winnetka, Illinois. She went to Northwestern University just miles from her childhood home and, like Lucy, her friends to this day remain the girls she met in grammar school.

Her best friend in the whole world is Noël, who we all call Noly. They met at summer camp in *third* grade and are now both divorced in their midseventies. They decided to move next door to each other and live in a classic colonial brick landmark, with huge white columns and just enough ivy, only blocks from Northwestern. It's a house split in half. Noly's home is to the left, and my mother's is to the right. Their sprawling apartments are adjoined by a porch, which they can each enter from their living rooms through a French door, and where they meet often for coffee or iced tea. They watch movies together, borrow soap from each other, swap stories of children and grandchildren, but mostly they have each other.

We grew up with Noly's five kids and went everywhere together: beaches, church, parks, parades, their house, our house, their street, and our street. When Noly got divorced, she didn't seem to mind much and carried on as usual. Several years later, my father left my mother, and my mother's heart was shattered into five thousand pieces. She had seven kids under the age of fourteen and they all expected life as they'd known it to resume. Of course, it never did.

Even with seven kids, rain, snow, and PTA, my mother

would gather bimonthly with her gang: Noly, Cookie, Mrs. Marin, and the then infamous Mrs. Morris, an eccentric woman who wore mounds of clanking bangle bracelets on each arm, and whose skin was so tanned year round, my brothers used to call her "the leather lady." She had a low smoky voice and eyes that saw right through you. This gang would saunter through our front door, lugging six-packs of Fresca and Tab, all smoking Kent cigarettes, shouting over one another. They would settle in our living room, talking, laughing, and sometimes even dancing. My mom would play the piano and they would sing and party. I would fall asleep with my bedroom door open on many a night to the sound of my mom's laugh roaring above the rest of them.

My mother's friendships and their importance to her affected all of us growing up. From the way she lived her life it was clear that the honoring of female friendship in our home was high on the value system. When I've asked her about her friendships and what she thinks may have helped so many last, she tells me that she doesn't question friendship, just as she doesn't question God. When I asked her about the few friendships in her life that had ended, she responded with Longfellow's words, "Thy fate is the common fate of all; into each life some rain must fall." Bad stuff will come our way. It's just rain; it's not to be probed or picked or stopped. I love that she has this attitude, but I still have to question the rain, and I have to know it can't be changed. I have found that the things we think we cannot change are so often things that we can.

Maybe a real etiquette that we could all actually follow without question could be something as simple as the truth.

CHAPTER NINE

Working:

Friendships—Two Sides of the Business End

S tanding in my living room one morning, I glanced out the window and watched a metallic mint-green Mercedes pull into our driveway. I walked outside and approached the quiet car. The driver, a casual friend of mine named Brooke, shot me a familiar smile and asked, "Like it?"

I leaned in the window and scanned the pristine cream leather interior of her new car. The tortoise-colored frames on her Chanel sunglasses were the exact color of her steering wheel.

"What's not to like?" I answered.

Brooke and I have known each other for a few years and had run into each other at a party a couple of weeks earlier, where she started to talk about a friend of hers at work. She was here to tell me more.

Brooke is the president of a $100 million corporation. According to Catalyst, a leading women's research and advisory organization, Brooke is in the rare 13 percent of women in this country who hold such positions in the corporate world. Her accomplishments single-handedly bumped up the statistics that track the financial success of women in America. She's also a happy wife and the mother of several children, which leaves her with little idle time.

Blond and great-looking, Brooke is always groomed and polished to the nines. She's probably near fifty, but you'd never know it. Brooke makes a point of letting you know what she does, who she is, and how she feels about things. She's spent the last twenty years of her life climbing to the top of a male-dominated corporate ladder.

"There's nothing like working in a den of lions all day every day, let me tell you. I've learned to play every role in the book. I'm the flirt, the mother, the vixen, the innocent—whatever it takes, I can do it, and it's why I am where I am. Men are tough, Liz, but women can be vicious."

"What do you mean?"

"Vicious, as in vicious. Some of the worst betrayal in my life has come from the women I've known. It must be the way it takes you so off-guard. See, men have been betraying women for centuries. Literature, movies, television, all have warned us to expect betrayal from men, but not so much from women. When a girlfriend betrays you, it's a shock; even if it's happened before, we somehow never expect it. And it cuts us in a different kind of way, as though it's not supposed to happen, you know?"

She continued. "Last year I had a national corporate meeting in New York. All my sales reps and team heads were going to meet, party, and go over annual production. We'd planned a dinner where we would honor those who had shown outstanding sales or management abilities. I hire all management in the Western region, and part of my goal has always been to try to infiltrate women into positions. My two top salespeople who live in different cities are women; I've known them both for more than ten years. I hired them at the same time, and the three of us over the years became great friends. Lisa is like the little sister I never had, and Carol is my confidante. She is sharp as nails and hungry to work and learn.

"They come to birthday parties for my girls; they call me when they're down, or swamped, or in trouble. They both celebrate an occasional holiday with our whole family, and through the years I've come to see them as the two people at my company I really care about.

"Anyway, the night of the big dinner arrived and I was rushing to get there in time. I had made a plan to meet Carol and Lisa beforehand for a cocktail. I wanted to show them pictures of the kids and let them in on a new idea I was working on for the company. The dinner was something all of us had been looking forward to. It was the first year we'd done it with awards and announcements of promotions, that kind of thing. We were always up for a way to get to New York together.

"I showed up for cocktails with the girls, we began with our standard office gossip, and then we toasted our all-time favorite city. The pictures came out, the kid-talk came up, and before we knew it we were heading into the dinner. Carol was praised and raised as we call it at the dinner and Lisa spent half the evening on the phone with her young daughter who was at home with the chicken pox.

"Just as the party was winding down, it began pouring rain. I mean torrential. We were trying to locate our cars, and the good-byes were a bit rushed. I'd asked Carol to call me if she had a second, I had one more thing I wanted to tell her. I then rushed to my car and waved good-bye as they got into their own car.

A few moments later my cell phone rang. I picked it up and said hello, but there was no response. I said hello again, and then I recognized Carol's voice. I also heard Lisa's voice, yet they weren't speaking to me, they were speaking to each other. I realized that Carol's phone had somehow inadvertently dialed mine. I couldn't help listening because they were talking about *me*. I might have thought to hang up when I realized they couldn't hear me, but I didn't. I proceeded to listen to these two friends of mine denigrate and criticize me . . . all of me. I listened until they were finished, which was about fifteen or twenty minutes."

I took a long moment and then asked, "What did they say?"

"What didn't they say?" she answered.

"Well, were they bashing you as a boss, or a worker, or a mother, or a friend or what?"

"All of the above." She was somber with this answer. As

much as I wanted to know details I could see she wasn't going to give them. They had cut hard through Brooke. We sat there quiet for a moment, and then I asked, "Well, what did you do?" Brooke's toughness reappeared.

"I am their boss, I *hired* them, I go to *bat* for them, I couldn't believe it. So I did nothing at first, I waited out the rest of the weekend."

"That couldn't have been easy."

"No, but I did it. And then early Sunday morning as we were getting ready to fly home, over coffee at the hotel I confronted them. I calmly recited every word that each of them had said about me, and then I added that I didn't realize they'd felt this way."

"Okay . . . did they say they were drunk? Or that you might have taken it out of context?"

"No, they weren't drunk, and there was no confusion as to the context, they had no defense."

"So what did they do?"

"What do you think they did? Both of them burst out crying and began apologizing. It was quite a scene. Look, this was hard for me. No, it was devastating. I had to work against all the emotion inside me, and make that confrontation, for the sake of work. I had to divorce myself in a moment as a friend and remain their boss. From the minute I heard them trashing me, they were not my friends, they were my employees and my coworkers."

"Did you tell them that?"

"No, I didn't have to."

"So, you got up and left and that was it? I mean you just never spoke to them again as friends?"

"Well, I wanted never to lay eyes on them again, the betrayal was that deep. I continued a working relationship and that was it."

"And did they just sort of follow your lead?"

"It was pathetic ass-kissing from them for a long time, but in fact Carol left the company soon after because she was offered a great position somewhere else. And a few months ago I actually hired her back. She is a fantastic salesperson who is gifted at this job."

"So it's that easy. Because it's work you just turn the emotions off?"

"No, not at all. This is very challenging for me. As often as I say, 'Hey, I don't have time for this crap,' I realize it's not about time, it's about how it makes you feel, and how you can't control that. I'm never easy with what's out of my control.

"The air is thick when I speak with either of these women, let alone both of them. The three of us along with two other men meet weekly, and just the other day I had to make a change on something Carol put together. She said to me after I made the changes that I didn't like her, or that I have problems with her. I looked right at her and said 'Listen, it's business, Carol. You didn't do this properly, and you need to fix it. It is *business*.' I'd be lying, Liz, if I said this isn't hard. Until today, I think I haven't been totally honest with myself. I've tried not to let it get in the way of my work, but I'm sure it does, more than I realize."

I wondered if this same scenario had happened with her friends *outside* of work, if she'd have handled it the same way. I asked her and she told me emphatically, "No, no way, because I wouldn't have had to. If I heard my two dearest friends saying the same awful things about me, well, I can barely think about that. But I imagine I would never speak to them again."

"Brooke, why? I mean why wouldn't you let them know you'd overheard them?"

"Well, I can't say I wouldn't for sure, but I don't think I'd tell them because it wouldn't matter. The friendship would be over."

"It was the worker side of you that was able to address them, then?"

"Oh, my God, yes. I was my complete work-self that morning for coffee. I played the role of tough, confrontational woman. I could *never* have done that with my regular friends. I cried my eyes out in the ladies' room that day after coffee. As brave and calm as I forced myself to appear, I was blown apart emotionally."

Brooke told me she had recently been invited to join nine other women who run corporations on a philanthropic board. These women pool their ideas, resources, and connections and raise funds for the needy. The magnitude of what they can accomplish among the ten of them for other people is beyond comprehension, she said, and she was clearly excited and proud to be doing it. When I asked her had she made friends with any of the other women on the board, she laughed a little, but after some thought, said, "Honestly, at this level among these women it becomes about who out-powers whom. In that room with those women, again, it's business. I am now relentlessly committed to being cautious before allowing a woman into my life, period."

Did she mean since her falling out with Carol and Lisa, I asked?

She answered, "Absolutely, since my falling out with them. It's sad, I think, because at the end of the day when we go home, there is no question that all of us want girl-friends, we want to have the chats, and we want to be liked, just like everyone else."

Even powerful women are not spared the heart-shattering experience of friendship ending.

After my talk with Brooke, I became extremely interested in friendships ending in the workplace, and wondered if they weren't in a category all their own. Even Brooke, who is uniquely qualified to confront and was the actual boss of both her friends, claimed that addressing her situation was one of the most difficult experiences of her work life. More common than Brooke's, however, were stories of women who had to show up every day at work, and see a now "for-mer" friend. Women use the silent treatment when they can't avoid someone.

Nancy, a bookkeeper at an insurance company in a small town in the South, told me about her and her friend Rachelle. The two of them decided "late in life," as she put it, to venture out into the workforce. Both of them were hired almost ten years ago, when they were in their fifties. They sat two cubicles apart and had had a fairly regular routine going on for years. They would meet at the train station each morning, bring their local papers and clip coupons, talk about their families, and discuss recipes for weekend get-togethers. They enjoyed their lunch side by side, and when work would pile up for one of them, the other would always pitch in to help.

One morning, Nancy showed up at the train station and Rachelle wasn't there. She waited until the last second and then got on and sat in their regular seat. Nancy recounted, "Normally, she would call and tell me if she was not going to be there." When she stepped off the train that morning, she noticed Rachelle stepping off another car at the opposite end of the train. She tried to wave to her but Rachelle didn't see her. At lunchtime that day, Nancy noticed that Rachelle quickly disappeared. After a few days of confusion, Nancy approached her.

"Rachelle was strange," said Nancy. "She acted as though she hadn't noticed the changes in our routine. I told her it would be nice if she would let me know ahead of time if she weren't going to be at the train station, and she told me she wasn't going to be at the train station anymore. I wondered if she was ill, but she looked fine. I told her I was sorry to hear that, and how much I enjoyed her company. That's the last time we've spoken, I think.

"My husband, who retired last year, is concerned. He says I'm not my joyful self when I return home in the evenings. And I don't feel joyful. I suppose I miss my friend. I do wish she would tell me if I've said or done something to make her not want to share our lives together." Then she asked me, "What do you think, dear? Do you think there's anything else I can do?"

I thought it was sad, pure and simple. She was lonely for her friend and wanted back what I guessed was not coming back.

"I think it sounds like you have done all you can do, Nancy. Rachelle might be going through something and perhaps later she will decide to share it with you. I know this can be very hard. Believe it or not, I've heard this kind of story often. Each one makes me sad. You're not alone in having suffered this."

"Yes," she said. "Well, it's also quite confusing."

I waited as she cleared her throat and then I asked her, "Are there any other women at work you might be interested in getting to know?"

"Oh, most of them are much younger than we are. I have other friends, but no one I get to see every day. I'm used to Rachelle. We get on so well, and we know how everything goes. My stomach hurts a bit every morning on my train ride, and often I'm not hungry at lunch these days. My husband thinks I should give my notice. I don't *have* to work. We'd be okay, but I've enjoyed it so much, and I don't know how I'll do at home every day. I've given some thought to helping a cousin I have, who owns a hair salon. In fact Rachelle and I have spoken many times about later on, working together a few days a week. The both of us have a knack for braiding. We practice all the time on the kids, but I don't know if I'd do it without her."

I couldn't try to guess what Rachelle could have gone through to end this sweet friendship, but clearly there was something. I shared a Kahlil Gibran quote with Nancy: "When you are sorrowful look again in your heart and you shall see that in truth you are weeping for that which has been your delight." She loved it and asked me to repeat the quote so she could write it down. Our conversation left my heart heavy.

Months later Nancy wrote and told me she'd finally quit her job. She'd been home several weeks and was joining a garden club. She is working for her cousin at the beauty salon every other Wednesday and enjoying it. She hadn't heard from Rachelle, but still thinks of her often.

Nancy's story is similar to that of Jackie, whom I'd met just days later. Younger than Nancy, Jackie is a single mother in her thirties. She and her friend Mara had been working next to each other as receptionists in a doctor's office for almost four years. They rode the bus in the mornings together, ate lunch at the same diner, and shared much of their lives as single mothers. Jackie spoke a lot about the stress of raising a child on her own, and how Mara had helped so often in times of need. Over the years they'd built a support system on which Jackie clearly counted.

Mara, out of nowhere, departed suddenly from Jackie's life, giving her the silent treatment. Like Rachelle, Jackie approached her friend with questions, and like Rachelle's friend, Mara was vague. It was so disconcerting and uncomfortable for Jackie to work next to her friend all day and not talk; she told me she called in sick several times. She claimed the people in the office were inquiring about it and affected by it—the nurses, the doctors, the waitress at the diner where they eat lunch together. Even Jackie's seven-year-old boy had begun to ask her why she was so sad all the time.

"It was like someone died. Maybe at some point I'll stop thinking about why this happened, but I know that I'm never going to stop missing her . . . and the fun she is. I felt so stupid about how hard I took it, like I shouldn't feel that crushed. I guess we were just great friends, real friends, and now we're not."

Finally after two months, Jackie went to her boss and begged to be transferred upstairs to an office in the same group of doctors but at a different location, separate from Mara. She told me she felt lucky to have had a woman as her boss, because when she was asked why she so desperately wanted a transfer, Jackie told the truth, and her boss confided that she had also recently gone through a similar experience. The two swapped stories and Jackie was transferred the next week. Clearly not everyone is able to remove herself from her position near a former friend, but it appears that when we can, we do.

Haddy also told me about her work friend.

"I met my friend Iris when I started work at Dottie's Delight, a diner near the freeway not too far from where I live. I've always waited tables. It's what I know and what I like, being around people and keeping busy. The only complaint I have is that it's starting to get hard on my feet." Haddy is past sixty, but looked much older to me. She told me she wouldn't feel right if her bones didn't feel tired. "It's all I know."

It's been two years now since she broke off her decades-long friendship with her pal Iris. They had done a lot of things together, from victory bingo nights, to long talks at the diner after work. She described Iris as the friend in her life with whom she'd shared the most about herself. "She's bossy, she is, but she knows how to have a good time." Then with determination she said, "You got to do what's right in life because you don't want to go out with too many regrets. Not long ago, I watched my father die of loneliness. He wasn't so much a sick man as he was a man who had nothing to live for. Watching what loneliness can do to someone is just about the most eye-opening thing a person can have happen to them.

"My mother, on the other hand, had a gang of friends; she called them her 'posse.' When my mom became ill years ago, I remember her posse like they were here yesterday. They were my mom's backbone.

"They brought the card games to the hospital and the hair gel to her bedside. They took care of my brothers, they fed my father, and every day they lit a candle at church. Every one of them let my mom know if she ever needed anything they were there. No one ever had to ask for a thing from this posse. The love and care these women showed my mother and our family stuck hard in me.

"You see, my friend Iris is a good woman. She really is. And at the time in our lives when we met, maybe we needed each other. We got very close very fast, and it felt just right. We spent most every day together in one way or another. People often thought we were sisters. Poker and bingo were our things, and the dollar store. We loved the dollar store. Iris had a tragedy with one of her daughters and together we got her through it. She's strong as an ox, Iris is. And she and my dad got on great.

"Several years after we met, when my dad started getting bad and needed me more, it was hard on me. I'd call Iris and ask about bingo or poker or whatever it was that night I would have normally done. And she'd tell me about it.

"The pictures in my head of my mom's posse kept appearing during that time, and then as I watched the lonely death of my father I started to feel the pain of my own loneliness. I had broken ties with many of the people in my life that I'd cared about. I got busy, I guess, and when I looked around all I could find was Iris. I will not speak ill of her because she is a good woman, but around the time my dad was bad, Iris was not there for me. Never did she offer a hand, not that I expected it, but looking back on it after Dad had gone, I realized Iris was not the friend I thought she'd be."

After she said this I thought of my own mother, who constantly reminds me how easy it is be kind and generous when times are fine, but the measure of a true friend is what happens when times are tough.

Haddy went on. "I stopped my friendship with Iris after Dad passed, and I started getting a hold of old friends I hadn't seen. I missed the people I'd let fall away, and I made it my business to try and bring them back." She took a breather, and I asked, "How did Iris take it?"

"Well, I just started doing my own thing. At first I thought she didn't notice, that's how she is, but . . . she did. She seemed sad at work for a while, and I thought if she does ask, maybe I'll tell her, but if she doesn't, I won't. And she never did. It was awkward, but I kept busy. One night I was closing up and noticed she was hanging around a little. I looked at her and said, 'What is it, Iris?'

"She looked back and said, 'I am sorry about your dad.'

"I said thank you and that was it. Sometimes you just got

to do what feels right. I don't want to die lonely, sweetheart. God bless her, but with a friend like Iris, I saw my life leading to a place I don't want to go."

Haddy told me it's been almost two years and both she and Iris still work the day shift at the diner. A part of her feels guilty for leaving the friendship, but as she put it, "A bigger part of me knew I had to do what was right for me."

CHAPTER TEN

Gram:

The Power of Regret

Many women, when deciding to end a friendship, move into a hidden, interior world. When we arrive there, we adopt a comfortable, casual sense of indifference and communicate with nuances of behavior, rather than the standard exchange of words. From this little world only we can see how we work to end a friendship and when we're finished, we move back out.

Maybe it's all an unconscious attempt to avoid the upheaval we know these endings will cause in our emotional lives. We separate ourselves from our usual emotions. But the little world can't keep you from the emotions and truth that live in your heart no matter how hard you try or where you go. They will always know how to find you and eventually they will.

I met Maria at one of my early discussion groups and couldn't get out of my mind the story of her ended friendship and the profound regret she felt. Maria and Nina had been friends their entire adult lives. Their relationship sounded mildly Thelma and Louise—describing their everyday lives as adventurous would be an understatement. Road trips to unknown destinations were a monthly ritual. They'd jumped out of airplanes together numerous times, and their idea of a fabulous Sunday afternoon was *tattoo* salon hopping.

Along with their passion for adventure, they were music maniacs. Nina was an amazing singer who would crash karaoke contests when her ego needed boosting. Almost every moment of the friendship Maria described was laced with something edgy or fantastic, although it was clear she didn't miss just the great times, she missed her friend.

Even though the friendship had ended, she soberly told me, Nina was her hero in all the ways that really mattered. She was honest and real—qualities that Maria coveted the most.

Maria shared everything in her life with Nina, and always felt safe. She told me, "Sometimes you look up and thank the universe for the things that come into your life. Years after I'd met her, while I was still her friend, I was always looking up and giving thanks for Nina."

Maria got engaged to her boyfriend, Joel, whose relationship with Nina was strained. "You know, the best-friend and the boyfriend thing, it's hard. Nina's known me longer and tends to feel she knows me better, and Joel thinks she's full of shit. Not so uncommon, right?" She was right. A lot of women go through this struggle when the man of their dreams begins to take over the heart and time of the friend.

After her wedding, Maria described herself as feeling as though she couldn't find a way to juggle or even try to balance Joel and Nina within her life. Something felt forced and unnatural, but instead of facing it and dealing, she did what she told me came easiest to her. She took the shortest road she knew and slowly vanished from her dear friend's life, without a word of explanation. It was hard, she told me, but not hard enough *not* to do it.

Still, it was gut-wrenching for Maria, who told me, "Time kept passing and, as much as I missed her, I didn't know what to do. I knew after a week I'd made a mistake; that I should have told her what was going on, and figured a way through it, but by then it was too late."

I asked her, "Too late for what?"

She was crying when she said, "Too late to take it back and make it okay."

Is it ever really too late to tell someone you're sorry, when you know you've done the wrong thing? But I think Maria meant that it was too late to change what she'd done; she felt she would never be able to take it back and have *that* friendship *that* way again in her life. Maybe she was right.

Maria said that she had only recently begun to realize the amount of denial she'd used to get her through this experience, because if she hadn't been denying how awful it was, she could not have lived with herself. It had been four years since she'd spoken to Nina when she told me this story, yet when she began I would have guessed less than a year. Her emotions were so raw.

Months after I'd met Maria, she called me and asked if I wanted to hear about the last chapter of her friendship with Nina. We met for coffee.

Maria explained that both she and Nina had a very close mutual friend named Tara, who had apparently remained true and there for both of them through the falling out. Interestingly, Tara had never once asked Maria why the breakup was happening.

At just about the five-year mark of their ended friendship, Tara got engaged. She called and asked if Maria wouldn't mind helping *Nina* plan the shower. Maria told her she was quite sure Nina would not agree to that, and Tara assured her she'd already checked, and it was fine with Nina.

The two old friends spoke for the first time on the phone. Maria was nervous but excited. When she heard Nina's voice, she swelled with memories and hope. But the second Nina realized it was Maria, her voice went stone cold. In that moment Nina told me she'd felt the lowest feeling she'd ever known inside herself. They struggled through together and eventually found a way to plan the shower. Anytime the conversation strayed to something remotely personal, Nina quickly steered it back to the shower plans. They spoke several times and it never got better. With each phone call, Maria became more and more overwhelmed with regret and shame.

Just before their friend Tara was to be married, Maria decided she was going to tell Nina everything, her regret, her apologies . . . all of it. She simply couldn't live with the situation as it was. Yet Maria was afraid Nina wouldn't agree to meet her, so she decided to write a letter.

Maria then recalled that when she was first at the discussion group at my house, she'd shared her story with all the other women attending, and was the only one who had initiated this kind of avoidance, the only one who had ditched and left her friend without a word of warning. The women who'd shared their perspectives from their side of the experience threw her completely with the intensity of their feelings, their pain and confusion. Yet a part of her envied them, because they didn't have to live with the kind of shame and remorse that comes with being the guilty party.

Now, Maria felt she needed to get it out ... to face Nina and tell the truth. But, she said, even the truth would not nearly make up for what she'd done.

Nina,

I had wanted to tell you this in person, as I thought I was going to be able to see you at some point alone ... in fact I've been wanting to tell you this for years. Feeble and weak as I have been, I have not.

But here goes. I say this to you with all that I am. I am sorry ... I am more than sorry for every second of my behavior that encircles the ending of our wonderful friendship. If I had it to do over again, I would never have done it! I've learned a lot about life and what matters since this happened, and must admit losing your friendship is one of the hardest lessons I've had to learn. I hope I have grown and changed since then.

All I can say in an effort to explain, as I certainly can't really defend my abhorrent behavior, is this. I was weak and wrong and couldn't seem to see clearly what the right thing to do was at that point in our lives. And I live with that with great regret.

As I write this I want you to know I don't imagine to gain forgiveness, I want only for you to know and believe that I am sorry. And for what it's worth I have never not thought of you. I've told my children of you. I've carried all the memories we shared together safely inside me as a part of who I am.

Everything we were as friends has never come close to repeating itself for me with another friend. I am so regretfully sorry . . . and am sure it can't be easy to speak with me, or think of me in a good way after what went on; with that I want you to know how much I appreciate how kind you are toward me.

So much life has happened for both of us in the last nine years. And I already see in the few short conversations we've had what a wonderful blessed and giving person you obviously continue to be. I think of myself as a heart-filled person, Nina, but when I think of how I handled our friendship I truly see how heartless I was . . .

Thank you for being able to take the high road to make this shower for Tara.

All my love,

Maria

Nina called Maria after she received the letter and thanked her. Maria told me she could never even try and explain the relief she'd felt and she wept with joy on the phone with her friend. They spoke for a long time. Nina held tough in saying how painful and unexpected Maria's behavior had been, and Maria responded by repeating how sorry she was and how she wished she had not done it. They spoke for the first time about their kids and family members and things they used to care about together. Nina was still the Nina she'd remembered, and in that hour they spent on the phone it was like old times.

Maria hopes slowly to earn back the trust of her friend, to get to a place where they can remain in each other's lives. Perhaps they can begin to be friends again, although she was sure it would never be what it once was.

Her letter had become the key to letting her out of the cell of regret she'd created for herself. With it, both friends felt their pain resolved and a measure of peace.

"Regret is insight that comes a day too late."

For some women, the chance to make it right never comes.

I was having tea in the dining room of an old hotel in Hollywood with Christine O'Malley, my friend Rooney's grandmother. She had phoned to invite me the day before. I was curious about why, since she and I had not seen each other without Rooney with us.

The first time I met Gram I was already engaged to my husband, Thomas. I'd been invited at the last minute to join the family for dinner because Thomas was stuck out of town on location. Gram was sitting on the couch quietly taking in the life of the room. She smiled at me and said, "Well, look what we have here. Sit down and tell me about yourself and your wise eyes."

I sat down and Gram and I became friends. She is a gem of a woman, an amazing soul with a lucid mind. She describes herself as a stubborn Irish broad, yet is one of the grandest, kindest, most humble human beings I've ever encountered. Gram and I are simpatica and have a mutual regard that leaves me feeling so damn good every time I'm with her. I like her and her sturdy sort of greatness. It's easy to forget when you're around her that she's closing in on her eighty-eighth year.

The day we met for tea, Gram was wearing a black velvet coat and hat, with a white silk scarf tied at her neck, and her signature Jackie O glasses, which she claimed to have worn since before Jackie was even born. An antique silver cane was propped against her chair. This woman had the kind of style one might expect from Hollywood royalty.

The dining room looked as if it had been preserved since the late 1940s. A beautiful array of silver tea carts lined the bank of French doors. Waiters in white gloves and tuxedos stood against the walls. Soft Mozart melodies played quietly throughout the room. The staff doted and fussed over Gram when we were served as I took in the peaceful view of the Hollywood hills.

Gram poured our tea, took a sip, and then looked up at me with her ice-blue eyes and said, "I've got a story for you. For your book. That is, if you want to hear it."

"Sure I do." I fumbled around for my notepad.

"When you were telling me about the women in your

book who wrote letters to each other, it got me thinking. Then I couldn't stop the thinking. I had a friend back a long, long time ago. She was the first real friend I'd ever had. Most of my close relationships were with my sisters and my relatives.

"When I met Fiona, it was a great day in my young life. I knew that second how lucky I was to cross paths with the likes of Fiona Langer. Once we got to know one another there was no stopping us. Our friendship soared and we soared with it. We gave each other confidence, and reason, and hope, the things you need when you're young. We were eighteen, both of us a little lonely and uncertain, living in New York City, looking for work in the theater. When one of us was down, the other would pick her up. Together, it was never too tough. Jobs were scarce, and our families were a long way away. We talked about politics and acting and poetry and philosophy. We went to the theater as often as we could afford, and afterward we would lie on our beds envisioning scene after scene until we'd memorized entire shows well enough to play them ourselves.

"Not so long after we met, we were at a party on Long Island. A friend of a friend invited us. We barely had the means to get there but we did. It was a huge, lush event, filled with interesting people. We made our way around the place, slightly intimidated by the grandeur. As we stood listening to the great band, two smart-looking gentlemen approached. They invited us to join them at a jazz club back in the city. We accepted and our tired lives took a sharp turn.

"Less than a year later we were engaged to be married,

both of us, to these men. Next thing we knew we were living in the same apartment building across the hall from each other, pregnant, and again sharing strife and hopes. Fiona was like a sister to me by then. I don't think I took a breath without letting her know I was doing it. We became women together, as we faced life. We gave birth and raised babies, we struggled through marriage and we reminded each other daily of the life we knew we still needed to live. Fiona's family had all gone back to England, where she hoped one day to visit. Between the two of us we eventually had seven children.

"One day, a very ordinary day, I was walking home from the market in the freezing cold of December. My children were with Fiona and my husband was in Cincinnati on business. I stepped off the curb with my bags of food and slipped right onto the street. My coat was soaked with mud and snow, my groceries flew everywhere. As I started to get up I felt this strong grip around my waist lift me to my feet. I turned around and there before me was the gentlest set of eyes I'd ever seen. A man with soft brown hair and a camel-hair coat smiled at me. We just sort of stood there and stared at one another, until I finally said, "Thank you." He gathered my things and helped me home.

"Have you ever been in love, Liz? I mean really in love?"

"Yeah."

"Well, I hadn't. And it was the end of one life and the beginning of another. I was twenty-five years old. I had three small children, and I spent the next few weeks secretly falling in love with the man on the street whom I was sure I couldn't live without. Irish and stubborn as I am, nothing was going to stop me.

"You can't begin to imagine what it was like in those days to make a life choice like this. When I first told Fiona the secret of my heart, I was terrified that somehow she wouldn't care for me the same way, and in a moment my fears were realized. Fiona was devastated. I knew I would have to leave my husband, and break up my family, yet I also knew it was the right thing to do. Fiona wept and pleaded with me not to do it. She reminded me of the vows I'd made to myself and my husband and God. She wept for my children, whom she told me would never forgive me. I left her there weeping that day, my heart so low. Somewhere inside I knew leaving Fiona would be the most difficult.

"Several months passed. Fiona and I were not speaking. I prepared for my departure. I was going west with my children and the love of my life. My husband took the news in stride, and in the end wished me happiness and good fortune.

"My departure day arrived, but Fiona wouldn't answer her door. I kissed a letter I'd written and slipped it underneath the door. My letter explained my love for her and the hole that would be left inside me with the knowledge that she no longer could see me as a person for whom she cared. At the end of my letter I transcribed an old quote we'd grown to love over the years: 'Your pain is the breaking of the shell that encloses your understanding.' We'd spent hours as young women dissecting this quote to get to its profound meaning. My heart settled in a place low inside me without Fiona in my life.

"I started over in California. My family welcomed me, my children thrived, and Pops, the one and only love of my life, became my husband. I began to live truthfully and feel from a place inside of me I always knew existed but hadn't known before. I was happy."

As Gram carefully spoke, I felt like I was catching little glimpses in her eyes of that twenty-five-year-old woman, even though her story was sixty years old. She continued steadily.

"I received a letter from Fiona several weeks after I'd arrived in California. I carried it around unopened for days. I knew her heart on this subject in my life, and somehow I couldn't bear to open that letter and read the disdain and disapproval I knew she felt. After a week I handed the letter to Pops."

"Did he open it, I hope?" I said.

"No. I told him to throw it away. As much as I loved her, I just couldn't willingly bring the judgment and condemnation into my home. And this is the part I want to discuss with you. When you first brought this subject to me, I listened, as you revealed what you'd learned about friendship and avoidance. I remember telling you I hadn't avoided any women in my life. Yet the more I thought about it, the more I realized that of course I had. Actually, I may have indulged in the ultimate avoidance by merely refusing to read Fiona's letter. Fiona had a direct link into my soul, that's how close we were, yet I made a choice to live a life with Pops. Fiona knew me so well that I was afraid that the written truth of her feelings about my life might actually threaten the road I had chosen. So I had Pops throw it away.

"And then he passed last year, as you know. God, I miss him. I finally got around to sifting through and clearing out his old things. I found a box in our basement. A silver box no bigger than a cigar box, piled with dust. There were letters in this box written to all four of our children. At the bottom of these letters was a letter for me. I opened it and he'd written":

My dearest love,
There are some things you just know when you love a per-
son the way I have you. If I pass first, I've left this for
you . . . for I know your heart still carries a pain. Live your
life without me, as you did with me, from the depths of
your truth. I will love you throughout eternity.
                                        Your man Sam

"Beneath his letter was the unopened letter from Fiona. Which is right here." She pulled it out and placed it on the table. It was opened. I looked at Gram and could see her eyes growing wet. I picked it up and read,

Dearest Chris,   *September 10, 1949*
God, how I miss you. I have so much to say yet I find it hard
to write the words . . . I wish we could speak. I am so sorry for
my behavior and my judgment of you and the choices you
made in your one and only life. I think it was very selfish of
me . . . my desire to keep you here in my life overcame me,
my desperation for you to remain just as you'd been in my
life all those years stands behind the false and empty judg-
ments I presented. You are my rock and I yours . . . remem-
ber? Forgive my lapse . . . my temporary insanity. I wouldn't
give up this friendship for anything in the world. Your happi-
ness and truth are all that you have. We both know that.
*   I desperately want to come see you. Bob says I could*

come for my birthday if you'll have me. I love you . . . all of you and I always will. Give the kids my love and please fill your heart with the knowledge that I could never choose to live my life without you.

> *You know where I am*
> *Love and apologies*
>
> *Fi*

"Gram . . . oh, my God. When did you open this?"

"Two days ago."

There was the longest silence ever and then, "I was able to track her down. I'd always sort of kept track of where she lived. I've just learned she passed about a month ago."

"I'm sorry, Gram."

"Yep, so am I." And then she pulled out a picture. Two young women stood in the front of the Empire State Building in sweater sets and long skirts. They were holding hands and laughing hard. They were so beautiful. I could see in that old faded picture the lightness of the blue eyes that I knew were Gram's. She was a knockout.

"So, my dear, you now have my story. Perhaps not the classic avoidance story, but avoidance none the less. My regret is terrible. My life missed Fiona. Maybe I felt if I had Sam, I couldn't have Fiona, when all the while I could have had them both."

"Surely you made other friends, Gram?"

"Well, of course, but none was even close to the likes of Fiona Langer."

Gram had a faraway look in her eyes as she glanced out

the window, and then she said, "I'm lonely, dear. Pops is gone. Most of my life is gone; sometimes I feel like I'm just waiting to die. You can't help going over the things you could have changed and the things you should have changed when your time comes near. My life has been grand and my regrets are few. Part of me thought this might be a story worth passing on. Maybe it could make a difference for someone." Gram and I sat as the sun started turning pink and orange over the Hollywood hills.

"For the record, dear, Rooney is Pops's granddaughter. Her mother was my fourth child born here in California. She knows some of this story, but not about Fiona."

Gram's story cuts through me. Almost at the end of her life, she describes her regret with profound clarity. I walked Gram to the hotel entrance and put her in a cab. I decided I would call her once a month and ask her to tea. Her story will live in my heart forever, and I feel sure it will enlighten many about the power of female friendship. Gram had a rich life, no doubt. But she carried an enormous loss with her through it all, one that didn't have to be.

How many friendships might have had last chapters that never played out? Why so often is it that we don't give the benefit of the doubt to those we love and cherish most? Gram wrongly assumed a lot when she refused to open Fiona's letter, only to learn, half a century later, that the support and love that only a true friend can give was standing by with open arms.

How many other letters are waiting to be opened, read, or mailed? Is it really so hard to know what to do?

We women live with such enormous responsibility and

expectations that maybe avoidance of our friends has come to be a knee-jerk reaction to all the "should's" we face in our lives. Maybe we want, in our friendships, *not* to have to answer to anything or anyone.

Yet, society's unwillingness to acknowledge the importance of friendship and its ending helps us create more of them. But ultimately it is *we*, in the quiet of our hearts, who choose this pain for ourselves. We don't have to do this. We can make certain difficult choices—taking time to explain ourselves to our friends—in order to avoid worse pain . . . lasting pain. Choices about friendships are rarely life or death, but we need to face them.

I'm reminded of an old saying that goes something like: "A person can search his whole life for an answer, to turn around one day and realize he's had it in his hands all along." Maybe we are meant to keep searching, and when we feel uncertain, we're supposed to look a little deeper.

CHAPTER ELEVEN

A Blessing:
Reuniting Fallen Friendship

I couldn't help thinking about my friend Lila as I heard Gram's story. A few months after tea with Gram, I would be facing my fortieth birthday.

The day arrived, and a quiet spa treat and lunch with my friends Cara and Rooney had been planned. The spa was a slice of heaven and afterward we headed to a great restaurant. To my surprise, several other girlfriends were already seated at the table when we came in.

Raising my mimosa I toasted all of my friends for taking the time out to celebrate, and then my cell phone rang. I had a feeling it would be Thomas, because he had contributed to the lunch some adorable coffee mugs with a baby picture of me on them, and a caption that read, "Forty and still a babe."

I answered the phone and said "Hello," and on the other end I heard, "Hi . . . it's Lila."

There was a very long pause before I said, "Lila?"

"Happy birthday, Lizzie."

"Lila." I hadn't heard her voice in ten years. I think I was in shock for a second and then suddenly I was wracked with all kinds of emotions.

"Well, how did you . . . how are you . . . When did you . . . are you in New York?"

"Yes, a few weeks ago I got a call from your sweet husband," said Lila. "He said it took several weeks to track me down. He told me about your book and how he thought our friendship had a lot to do with you wanting to write it. I guess the stuff he read about the two of us just made him feel he had to call me. He told me he felt it was the best present he could think of. God, Liz, I've missed you. Thomas was so cute, he said he didn't know what my feelings were about you, and then asked if I wanted to call you there at the restaurant where you would be celebrating your fortieth birthday with friends. I've been carrying your cell number around for days with me. I could barely wait. So here I am."

I was speechless for a second. Thomas had contacted her? My head was reeling. He'd never even mentioned her to me. In fact, I remember after he read our story wondering why he hadn't said anything, or commented on the friendship, which he really didn't know very much about. Tears started pouring out of me. I couldn't stop them.

"Liz, are you there?"

"I'm here. God, Lila. Wow, thank you for calling." The polite WASP in me asserted itself even during this onslaught of emotion. Then I excused myself from the table and headed out of the restaurant. All of my friends had known that Lila would be calling. I found a quiet spot in the parking lot and sat there on a curb for forty-five minutes talking to Lila on the cell phone. We covered a little of bit of everything. She told me she'd been through some major changes in her life. And it would mean more than anything to her if we could be back in each other's lives.

"I want our friendship back, Liz. I miss you." The whole thing was perfect . . . and huge. She told me I better get back to the restaurant. I hung up with the promise that we would speak soon. It was like getting hit by a Mack truck emotionally. I stood in the parking lot for a second trying to gather myself. Then I called my husband and told him what a great man he is.

I was elated. I walked back into the restaurant and looked at my good friends and the mugs and I thought about Lila. Nothing could have made that day better.

The following week, I saw Lila for the first time in ten years. Her husband had business in L.A. She flew in, got a car, and came straight to my house. I felt like a first-grader the night before Christmas as I waited for her to arrive. She walked through our front door and we both screamed and hugged and laughed. There wasn't an ounce of weirdness or hesitation. She looked identical to how I'd remembered her. We were both wearing blue jeans, T-shirts, and cardigan sweaters. She was 1,000 percent Lila. She hugged all my kids and showed us pictures of hers. She also had three, and they were about the same ages. After she left that day, my son Augie asked me, "Mom, is she one of your sisters?"

"No, honey, I told you, that's Lila. Remember, we were friends when I was really young? I've known her almost forever."

Augie looked like he was thinking very hard and then said, "Why is she so much like you?"

"I don't know, buddy. I guess 'cause I've known her so long."

Lila and I saw each other every day while she was in Los Angeles. She would come in the mornings and stay all day. We took my kids to school, shopped, ate, and mostly just hung out and talked. One day we headed back to her hotel, and for the first time since I became a mother I stayed away for eight hours and almost forgot I had a family. We holed up in her fancy hotel and ordered room service and talked and talked and next thing I knew it was dark and late and I had to go.

After our three days together, it hit me hard. No friend in the world is like Lila. Maybe it was all the history coming back to us, but everything felt kicked up a notch.

She was soon on an airplane back to New York. The only sadness was knowing how much I would miss her in that everyday kind of way. We became e-mail junkies and phone freaks and now speak almost every day. Lila is back in my life full force. We have found as many opportunities as we can to see each other. We are utterly obnoxious to those around us when we get together for any length of time. That is who we are, Lila and I.

We eventually discussed what happened, but not immediately. On the day of our reunion, the anticipation was overwhelming. We were beyond elated, both of us, to be reconnected again and we were so busy in the amazing moment that we drew it out for as long as possible. However, we also shared a palpable sense of regret. The fourth time we saw each other, we made our way to addressing the new baby elephant in the room. How and what made this happen to *us*?

Lila initiated the conversation, and it began as the war of the apologies. A good amount of "No, I'm sorry," "No, I'm sorry," and then Lila forced me to shut up so she could say something.

She told me she'd been going through a lot of changes in her life, just before we reconnected. After living through the tragedy of 9/11 in New York City, she had begun to feel a shift in herself, one that was forcing her to look more carefully at who she was and who she wanted to be. She said, "I never answer my phone, Liz, *never*. I always let the machine pick up. That's just how I do it. So one night I was sitting outside on my tiny porch, for some reason I was alone, no kids, no nothing. I was sitting in the dark, filled with questions about my life and where I was, when the phone rang. I have no idea in the world why I would have picked it up, especially on that night, but I did. I said hello, and a man said, 'Lila, you are one tough person to track down. This is Thomas, your friend Liz Pryor's husband.'

"Liz, I swear to God I was speechless, and I have to tell you for a second I thought it was going to be bad news. I thought you'd been in an accident or something. And then, when he so gently asked me if I might want to get in touch with you for your birthday, I got so emotional. I don't know if he knew . . . but I did. Do you not think it's crazy that ten years go by and on the night I am contemplating the true meaning of life, your husband calls? I will never forget the feeling of knowing this was the plan, the big universal plan for me. The opportunity to change my path. I am stubborn and I shut things and people out when I don't know what to do. That's what happened to us. That letter you wrote me, you know I still have it. And, Liz, it is so beautiful and powerful. There's nothing I can say even to myself about the fact that I didn't respond to you. I don't want to be that person. I'm not that person any longer. That is the part of me that has brought most of the pain and sadness to my life, the part that needs to shut off and disconnect. Instead of dealing, I run, and I'm done running.

"Don't think I wasn't scared to death that you might have been so angry and hurt you would reject me; in fact I was totally prepared for that. But I knew I had to do it, and when I finally found the nerve to reread your letter after all that time, a part of me felt there was a chance, a miraculous chance that all of what you said could still be.

"When Thomas gave me your cell number to call on your birthday, it was still two weeks away. I was so anxious I went over and over in my head how it might play out. I carried your number with me like it was some kind of lifeboat. Almost as if I'd lost it, I would lose you . . . it was crazy. And all the while you had no idea of anything. I was petrified when I picked up the phone that day . . . that you'd be like, 'Yeah, what?' This was a huge ten years to miss, Liz, you know? We had kids . . . we're old . . . and I've really missed you."

I sat there and thought before I said anything. Lila was clearly trying to take full responsibility for what had happened, and I had to find my way to understanding, and then telling her my part in it, because we were both responsible. The letter I'd written her was really more of a covenant for the boundless love I was sure our friendship would hold no matter who or what came into our lives; we would hold this gift until the end of time. I remember how devastating it was to have felt none of it held true for her. But I also knew Lila, her way of dealing . . . as a girl and a woman she had been one to disappear when things got tough.

I then reminded her that she had called *me* two years after she received the letter, and tried to reach out to me. She had sent me a picture of her firstborn child and I did not call after I received it. She had picked up the ball, and I hadn't even tried to catch it. I had her number in my book the entire ten years . . . but I didn't use it. Not because I was angry, but because it felt so huge. I think a sliver of me was convinced she hadn't felt about me the way I had her, and it was too much for me to admit. Leaving it open was easier for me to accept; that way I could always hang on to the possibility that *I* was *her* Lila. When I told her all this, she cried . . . and then I cried. And then she said to me, "This will never happen again, you know that, right?"

And I did. Lila had clearly reached a turning point. Her willingness to look at the part of herself that helped make this happen was huge to me. Now I know I can trust her completely. I felt I could put my whole heart in her hand that day, and never fear she would drop it.

Through some miracle we have cut straight back into who we are to each other. We continue at times to touch on our decade of estrangement. I never know when or why it surfaces but it does, enough to remind us that we allowed it to happen. Everybody has her stuff, her baggage, her crosses to bear. It takes a lot to survive emotionally in this world. Lila ran, and I denied, and the combination hurt us both. But there is such a clear difference in where we both now live inside each other and it's great.

I invited Gram to tea at the grand old Hollywood hotel several weeks after reuniting with Lila. We sat in that beautiful dining room and I shared with her the Lila story from the beginning. She listened and wept a little, and then I showed her a picture of us that Thomas had taken on her recent visit to my house. We were sitting on the steps outside my bedroom door, Lila was looking at me, and I was looking at the camera. Both of us were laughing with our arms entwined. Gram looked at the picture and smiled a faraway smile. As she left that day, she gave me a big hug.

A few weeks after my tea with Gram, I found a letter in my mailbox. It was a small, cream-colored envelope with the letters *C.O.* embossed in the seal. I smiled as I opened it and read,

> *Dear Liz,*
>
> *I want to thank you for your company at tea. You have no idea of the joy it brings this old soul of mine. I also felt like sharing a few words from an old book I found written by Charles Caleb Colton: "True friendship is like sound health. The value of it is seldom known until it be lost."*

*Keep writing the truth of your heart, dear, for with it
will come peace.*

Love from your friend,

Gram

A few weeks after I got Gram's note, I received a call from
Rooney, who told me Gram had passed away. Beneath my
sadness that I would never see or speak with her again, a
part of me smiled for her because I knew she had been
ready to meet her end.

I have spoken to hundreds of women, and at the core of all
of their stories and emotions is the importance of truth—
the kind of truth that lives inside us every hour of every day,
where we know to look to see who we really are.

Stories of friendship elicit an almost contagious sort of
truth-telling from women. One confession would lead to
several and then to hundreds. Initially, perhaps, we were
commiserating with each other, but the friendship forums I
started became places where women talked freely and
frankly. Maybe they just needed a place to say something, or
maybe it's just because I asked!

The single most common statement I heard throughout
this process of discussing our friendships was, "I wish I
knew the right thing to do." The question of what was the
"right" thing to do came up in every note I received, on
every tape I made, and in every discussion I attended. In

fact, *The Right Thing to Do* could have been the title for this book. The law, religion, marriage, therapy, fashion—all of these social protocols guide us to make the right choices in our lives. Whether we consciously think about them or not, they quietly set our standard for decency. No matter how loosely implied or strictly enforced, they're there.

Yet there are no cultural, legal, or customary guidelines for what happens at the ending of a friendship between two women. This vital relationship has somehow slipped through the cracks. No right and wrong seems to guide us at this juncture. The only guidance we have is the truth that lives within each of us. Our challenge is to find it and learn to listen to it, and not just at the endings but at the beginning and throughout the friendship.

We've all experienced difficulties in our friendships. We'll have the occasional exchange that suddenly gives us a lump in our throat, a churning in our gut, a sweeping feeling of uncertainty. Just for a second you question everything about who your friend is, and then the feeling's gone. For one reason or a million reasons we decide to let it slide and, magically, that feeling disappears and the friendship continues without even a pause. *Those* are feelings of truth. Those are our instincts sending messages to which we need to pay attention.

If at the beginning of a friendship we listen to these messages a bit more carefully, we can learn to *acknowledge* and discuss them. Or, we shift, move or pull back, or bow out before the friendship becomes established. We can prevent an ending.

These women's stories will help me remember how I'd

like to live my own life. They testify to the importance of friendship and the significance of its endings. We owe it to ourselves and to each other, as well as to the girls who are on their way to becoming women, to look more carefully at the choices we make and the effects they have.

An ancient Chinese proverb says, "Tell someone something and they'll forget, show them and they may remember, involve them and they'll understand." I have watched as the process of telling the truth about our friendships has brought relief, emotional healing, and peace to the women who became involved in it. I hope that reading about them will help you in your life. I hope that you will go out into the world and talk about your own experiences with your friends, that you'll ask questions and listen to their stories. All it takes is asking. And as we open up to each other, society will have to notice. The shift has already begun with the women involved in this book. But as we begin to put on the map the effects of friendships and their endings on women, it will not be society that dictates the rules, but all of us women, because we'll be right here to do it.

There is great power in women banding together and talking about a subject close to our hearts. It feeds our souls, and can effect change. By simply talking to each other, we can bring honesty and recognition to an experience about which up until now we have remained silent, sad, and shameful. We can change that with acknowledgment and truth.

May you always remember the joy and contentment that your women friends bring to your life, and the honor that deserves.

ACKNOWLEDGMENTS

For a person to believe that she has something important to say, and then hope to get it out in the world is just a hope, until it happens, and then it's just amazing. I am overwhelmed with gratitude for the constant stream of open-minded people who surrounded me during the writing of this book. I want to thank all the women who shared their stories, my friends, my family, and the decision makers in the book world, whose faith in this subject helped pave the way through this incredible journey.

They include: my husband, Thomas, who chose me in this world to love, whose own passion for perseverance and individuality taught me more than he'll ever know. He is my knight, and together we are everything we need. And my children—Conner, Augie, and Luca—who now define my heart and my truth, I thank them for coming into this world and inspiring me to become who I was meant to be.

My father, Lee Pryor, for always showing me his faith in who I am, and for teaching me when I was young about the small things in life . . . that later became the big things. My stepmother and mentor, Julie Smith, for standing by me every second of this crazy journey with undying support and enthusiasm. Judy Proffer, for believing in something when it was nothing, for her overwhelming generosity . . . and for giving me a column in her paper without blinking an eye. Robin Borim for telling me to write this book, and for her confidence in who I am.

My brother Bill and my sister Alex, for reading my work and believing in me when I wasn't sure I believed in myself. My brother John, for the generous love he has shown me ever since I can remember. My sister Kiley, for teaching me about courage and reminding me about faith. And my sisters Jennifer and Tory, for their love and greatness.

My agent, Gail Ross, for coming onto my Web site and selling this book. Her creative director, Howard Yoon, for his sound judgment, and for making me feel like I had important things to say. My editor, Leslie Meredith, who is not only smart beyond smart, but whose kindness and faith in this subject has filled my heart and made this an amazing experience. And Carisa Hays, who took me under her wing and proved to be the greatest publicity director an author could dream to have.

To Lizzie Duncan, Sara Gooding, Laurie Guthrie Sykes, and Kristen Trucksess: you are the glue that holds me together, you are the angels of my life. Thank you for our friendship.

And finally, to all the friends I no longer have, with sadness and a new sense of clarity, I thank you for inspiring this journey.

INDEX

ABOUT THE AUTHOR

LIZ PRYOR grew up in a small suburb outside Chicago, with a passion for music and writing. She had aspirations of fiction writing upon leaving the journalism program at Kansas University. In her early twenties, Pryor supported herself by modeling for catalogs, local magazines, and acting in TV commercials. In 1990, the acting work took her to Los Angeles, where she continued to study writing at UCLA. She has spent the last decade committed to writing music, fiction, and nonfiction while being a busy full-time mom. Pryor's series, "Friendship Matters," originally written for the Sun newspapers, was sold to the new national women's magazine *Violet,* which debuted in April 2005. Liz presently lives in Studio City, California, with her three young children and husband, Thomas Calabro, a professional actor.

If you want to share a story, ask a question, or read more of Liz's work, please visit her at www.lizpryor.com.